D1167896

THE PRO'S EDGE: Vision Training for Golf
Dr. Lawrence D. Lampert

Dr. Lampert's vision training program is recognized and praised by vision experts, professional golfers, and professional athletes from across the country.

"Great golf tips for players at all skill levels. Expect higher level play with more satisfaction and consistently better scores from the application of his techniques."
– Dr. Michael Pier, Bausch & Lomb

"Great book . . . that can benefit every golfer at any level."
– John Nelson, Nelson's Golf Schools
1997 South Florida PGA Teacher of the Year

"Great book for the golfer wanting to learn golf from a different angle on the game."
– Judy Alvarez, LPGA/PGA Golf Professional

"I have searched the country for the answers Dr. Lampert provided in just one visit. Dr. Lampert's eye exercises are specific to my performance as a professional golfer."
– Patty Jordan, LPGA/PGA Golf Professional

"Vision training is a real eye-opener. Using the techniques in my instruction at our golf schools has really given the students and myself the pro's edge."
– Charlie Rulapaugh, PGA Teaching Professional,
Nelson's Schools of Golf, United States Schools of Golf

"Dr. Lampert's visual training ideas have undoubtedly made me a much better putter. I now have confidence to know that all of my five- and six-foot putts are going in the hole."
– Jack Shoenfelt, PGA Golf Professional

"The Pro's Edge: Vision Training for Golf *is an excellent resource for any golfer or optometrists interested in golf through vision training. This will definitely be part of the training golfers will be receiving in my office."*
– Paul Berman, O.D., F.A.A.O.

"I thank God for vision training and Dr. Larry Lampert."
– **Tony Fernandez, Cleveland Indians**

"Dr. Lampert's vision training improved my vision and depth perception on the playing field."
– **Hensley "Bam-Bam" Meulens, Arizona Diamond Backs, formerly Montreal Expos**

"I improved my tracking and control of my eyes in just a few sessions. I realized I had been overlooking one of the most important parts of athletic training—vision. Thank you for helping me visualize a dream."
– **Doug Jennings, formerly Chicago Cubs**
Currently holds MVP and consecutive home run record in the Japanese Baseball League

The Pro's Edge:
Vision Training for Golf

The Pro's Edge:

Vision Training for Golf

By

Dr. Lawrence D. Lampert

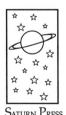

SATURN PRESS

The Pro's Edge: Vision Training for Golf
Copyright 1998 Dr. Lawrence D. Lampert

Cataloging in Publication Data available from Library of Congress.
ISBN: 1-885843-06-2

All rights reserved. No part of this book may be reproduced or transmitted in any form or by any means, electronic or mechanical, including photocopying, recording or by any information storage and retrieval system without written permission from the publisher, except for the inclusion of brief quotations in a review.

Printed in the United States of America

Cover design by Lightbourne Images, Inc.
Interior art by Visual Graphics, Inc.

Published by:
Saturn Press, Inc.
17639 Foxborough Lane
Boca Raton, FL 33496

Dedication

This book is dedicated to my wife, Lynn.
To my children, Paul and Hailey.
To my staff, Wendy, Leah, Liz, Maureen, Silvia, and Mary.
To my parents, my wife's parents, and finally to my patients.

Acknowledgments

I would like to thank my wife, Lynn, who I love dearly and who typed this for me and let me clutter up the dining room table for the many months it took to write this book. Also, my children Paul and Hailey. I love them dearly and their patience allowed me the time on the weekends to do the work. And then there is my staff—Wendy, Leah, Liz, Maureen, Silvia, and Mary—who are the heart and backbone of my practice and are like my second family.

Also, I'd like to thank my parents. I especially appreciate the experience in my father's optical office. Lynn's parents, Harold and Helene Rosen, were always there with their never-ending support and encouragement.

I also feel indebted to my patients who have chosen me as their eyecare physician out of all the other doctors available.

And where would we be without our teachers, our mentors, our colleagues. These people taught me to develop and grow in the science of Sports Vision. I would like to thank Drs. Al Sutton, Marty Birnbaum, Bob Sanet, David Cook, Craig Farnsworth, Dan Fleming, Don Getz, Dave Garfield, Bill Harrison, Brian Coffey, and Paul Berman for their inspiration. I would also like to thank Robert Krakow.

Finally I would like to thank my editor, Erica Orloff, and Kathy and Marc Levinson of Saturn Press.

Preface

If golf is a thinking person's game, this book will give you new things to think about. You will learn new information about your own vision system. Do you know if you are right- or left-eyed and which eye should be positioned over the ball? Do you know if you judge your target short or long or to the left or right of where it really is? Are you properly aligned for your long game? Are you sure your club face is really aligned with your target from the address position or do some of those easy putts miss to the right or left of the hole? Just reading this book will give you information you have never been given before and allow you to play at your best more often. If you do some work and master all of the concepts and procedures and use the exercises in this book, I guarantee you'll take strokes off your game. This is stuff many golf pros don't teach you unless they're affiliated with someone in sports vision training and most are not.

I recently attended a golf clinic. At the putting clinic, the two pros demonstrated the pendulum swing and how to consistently stroke the ball to the same distance each time. They stated that beyond that, putting was very simple as there are only two things to it—distance and direction. A woman with a puzzled expression on her face asked, "How do you know the speed and direction to hit the ball?" The reply was "That's judgment." This book will give you the technology to master that "judgment" and improve consistency from hole to hole, green to green. We will spend a significant amount of time on putting as I believe the short game is where you have the most potential to improve your score quickly. How many of you spend as much time practicing putting as you do on the driving range?

You will learn how to assign a different visual "target" for your putt and it's not the hole. Is every 15-foot putt the same? No, it may be uphill, downhill, or have breaks. So although the hole may be your destination and a most inviting visual target, it most likely will not be your visual target. You will learn how to reference your putt to a straight putt on level ground by "massaging" the green with your eyes for the right visual target. You will discover how long it takes for the ball to travel from putter to cup to aid you in "how hard" to stroke the ball.

This book contains eye exercises designed to improve your ability to read the greens, know the exact distance to the hole, and improve strength, flexibility, and stamina of your eyes so they don't tire and cause careless mistakes and miscalculations especially towards the end of a round.

I also detail procedures to sharpen your visualization and concentration skills so you can more consistently put yourself into "the zone" and not just happen upon it. You will know what "the zone" is and how to get there. I also include information about the right glasses, bifocals, and contact lenses for golf. So spend a little time with this book and discover one of the most exciting things to happen in golf in the last 20 years. Discover what big-money players are calling "seeing the line." This is the technology that has been mentioned on CNN and ESPN, in *Golf Digest*, and by announcers during golf tournaments. Sometimes this is the pro's "best-kept secret." Some players have made me agree to keep my work with them a secret as they consider it a competitive edge against the player who does not know about it.

My suggestion is to read the book cover to cover, then go back through it and do it step by step. At the end of each chapter, you will also see a "Hole in One" box. These boxes summarize what you will learn in each chapter. They are also a great way to skim through the book and find the parts that initially interest you the most. They quickly and concisely "refresh" key ideas to review periodically before you hit the links.

So take this journey with me and find your golf game magically transformed. You are about to learn *The Pro's Edge*.

Contents

Chapter 1
What is Vision Training?.. 1

Chapter 2
Who Does Vision Training? 11

Chapter 3
Self-Test: Your Visual System 15

Chapter 4
Alignment 33

Chapter 5
Distance 51

Chapter 6
Reading the Greens 61

Chapter 7
Find a Different Target 75

Chapter 8
The Mental Game 87

Chapter 9
Glasses, Contacts, Bifocals and Golf 101

Chapter 10
Eye Workouts and Programming 111

Chapter 11
Putting It All Together.. 125

Chapter 12
Your Personal Golf Journal 129

About the Author 147

Index 149

Chapter 1

What is Vision Training?

Your Visual System

Your visual system is linked to your brain in intricate ways that influence everything you do—including your golf game. Sports vision training is revolutionizing the sports world by using eye exercises to develop your visual skills to improve performance, consistency, accuracy, and stamina of your visual system. This gives the sports vision golfer an edge over golfers without this training and translates to improved scores.

What are visual skills? These include eye-hand coordination, speed and accuracy of eye movements, focusing, depth perception, judgment of location and reading contours, to name just a few. These all add up to being in "the zone," discussed in later chapters.

My first exposure to sports vision training was in relationship to hockey players. That made sense. The puck moves quickly and the players move quickly so it is a visually demanding sport. But it was obvious to me right from the beginning that I could train tennis players, baseball players, basketball players, race car drivers, skeet shooters, boxers, football players, and of course golfers. All the golfers I work with are very excited when they learn these techniques as they are specifically applied to golf. They get even more excited when they see these new skills improve their golf scores very quickly.

1

Sports Vision and Your Golf Game

What golfers usually find when they start sports vision training is that, prior to training, they tend to misjudge short or long or to the right or left. After you read this book, you will learn to make accurate judgments and assign a target for every shot. On the green, your target will most likely *not* be the hole itself. You will also learn how to accurately judge distance for all shots. You will master club face alignment so that you have the proper alignment over the ball. I view golf, to a large extent, as a target sport, except that you have two targets. One is the ball itself being struck by the club. The other target is where you want the ball to end up.

This book is well-suited to the average golfer as well as the pro. In fact, I often find the average weekend golfer stands to shave the most strokes from his or her score. I have even seen golfers improve dramatically after applying just one or two tips from this book. Golfers will also tunnel their vision when they are stressed and not relaxed on the course. This book can increase your relaxation dramatically.

Sports Vision: From Ball Sports to Running

Pro-ball teams are using sports vision professionals to evaluate and assess prospective draft choices. Sometimes they will choose a player with better visual skills over one who can run a little faster. One professional I know who does this told me he's met running backs who can complete six eye movements in one second. Right now, try looking back and forth from one object to another six times—and then see if you can do it in one second! The point is that elite athletes and pro golfers have elite vision skills. The average person can develop better visual skills to help them on the course, too.

In the summer of 1996, I was privileged to be one of the eye-care specialists who staffed the Bauch and Lomb Olympic Vision Center. The athletes took 12 standardized tests of sports vision skills such as dynamic visual acuity (seeing letters on a rapidly moving chart), eye-aiming ability, speed and accuracy of depth perception, eye dominance, eye-hand coordination, eye-hand and eye-foot response speeds, peripheral (side vision) awareness, and more. What was interesting to me at the Olympics was that the skills that an athlete excelled in visually pertained to his or her sport. For example, I found that many runners did not have great hand-eye coordination skills or contrast sensitivity as opposed to the kayakers who had great contrast sensitivity and hand-eye coordination. Kayakers must sense visually subtle patterns in the water and react quickly with their hands. Runners are not using this eye-hand connection unless they are passing a baton. But the runners had great side vision so they could see their lane and opponents without moving their eyes. Moving the eyes to look for lane markers or other runners slows a runner down.

After spending many years immersed in sports vision training, I have pinpointed those skills necessary for individual sports. So, what visual skills do golfers need?

1. Good eye-aiming ability. If this skill is not accurate, you will misjudge short or long or to the right or left of a target.

2. Depth perception. This aids in judging the distance and speed you have to hit the ball.

3. Eye dominancy. This is important for the position you adopt over the ball. It also aids in localizing where the ball really is and reading greens. Golfers who plumb bob with their right hand when they are left-eyed have problems. More on this later.

4. Eye-hand coordination. The eyes tell where the ball is and the arm and hands swing the club. Miscommunication between the two adversely affect your game.

5. Visualization skills. This is the ability to use your mind's eye to plan your shots.

Less important to golf are dynamic visual acuity (reading moving eye charts), because the hole is not a moving target; and speed of eye movements because in golf you have plenty of time to use your eyes and judge a shot.

My Model of Sports Vision Training

Level-One: Awareness

Sometimes I find increasing your knowledge about your visual system is enough to help your golf game. I have worked with a number of elite golfers who were greatly relieved when they had a reason for a problem they had been having.

I recently had a consultation with Patty Jordan, an LPGA touring pro. She told me she was having putting problems. She looked at the hole, looked at the ball, and when she looked back at the hole, it seemed to be in a different spot. When I checked her eye alignment (you will do this later), I found that her eyes tell her brain that the hole is closer than it really is and this "misjudgment" changes as she looks at the hole over and over again. She confirmed this by stating that many times her putts missed short. She also had trouble reading breaks. When we met, she was relieved to find an eye doctor who could identify her problem and was even more relieved to learn that her eyes, indeed, were playing tricks on her. Later, you will test your own eye alignment and learn the solutions to this particular problem.

Eye dominance is very important in golf and the information you will gain from my book may drastically improve your game. Just because you're right-handed doesn't mean you're right-eyed. In golf especially, eye dominance is critical to your position over the ball, especially in putting. Your head position is also key. This information is also invaluable when reading the greens.

Level Two: Defining and Testing Visual Skills

Eye Alignment

This tells us whether your eye muscles want to pull your eyes in or out from their alignment. Eye alignment relates to judging or localizing things as closer or farther than they really are. This is very important for golf and we will test this and train it later.

You may be aligning in front of, behind, or to the left or right of your target. You won't notice this without training . . . you won't experience double vision, but poor eye alignment is one of the most common causes for misjudgments.

Eye Movements

After reading this book, you will know how to move your eyes smoothly so you can run your eyes over the green to read the greens, judge the distance, speed, and path of your putts, and see the "line" so you can assign a target that is different from the hole at which to aim your putts. The average golfer really does not move his or her eyes along the greens from the ball to the hole to gain all this information. You will use smooth eye movements to visualize the path and trajectory of the ball for your long game.

There are two types of eye movements we analyze:

- Pursuits: This is a smooth following eye movement like watching a bird fly across the horizon.

- Saccade: These are movements where we rapidly shift our eye from one object to another.

Eye Focusing

Eye doctors call this accommodation. It is your ability to make your eyes see clearly from far to near and near to far. Unfortunately, as we age this becomes more difficult and we need bifocals. If your golf scores have gotten four to six strokes worse over the years, you will probably find that doing this program helps you regain that lost ground. You will learn skills to compensate for the loss of focusing—the same skill training the aging pro knows and uses.

This skill is important in golf especially for putting. The decline of this skill in older golfers usually coincides with decline in putting skills. This is another reason why aging golfers especially want to do this program.

Eye Teaming

This is your ability to keep both eyes working together and aligned in all different positions and at all different distances. When we train this system we usually improve depth perception, spatial localizations (where the ball is), and contrast sensitivity (important for reading the greens, see next section). Another reason to train eye teaming is that this eye system fatigues easily causing judgments to become inconsistent. This skill is very important in golf whether on the fairway or on the greens.

Contrast Sensitivity

This is the ability to see subtle differences against a background such as a ball against the dome or golf ball against the sky. I feel improving this skill improves reading the greens. After completing this program, you should start to see subtle rolls in the greens and directions of the grain—is it slow or fast, wet or dry? On longer shots, this will help you evaluate how the ball will roll once it hits the ground.

Depth Perception

This skill is the ability to judge distance of stationary objects and speed and direction of objects in motion. If you have average depth perception, you can demonstrate the lack of it to yourself by playing catch with a friend with one eye closed. Use a tennis ball to see what it's like. You can adjust to it, but then have your friend change the speed and arc of the ball. Now cover the other eye and try it. Next go back to using both eyes. This should be easier. Depth judgments are important in golf to judge the distance to your target on the fairway, distance to the green, and distance to the hole. Depth judgments can also change if you are looking up or down a hill. Improving this skill will also help golfers with one eye significantly weaker than the other or who have lost sight in one eye.

Peripheral Vision

This is the ability to see objects and motion out of the "corner of your eye" or with your side vision. You can train your eyes to see further out to the sides. In golf, this system will help you read the greens and judge the overall contours of each hole as well as aid with alignment for the full swing.

Training peripheral vision also aids in relaxation and concentration during the game. Peripheral vision expansion is like the relaxation response for your visual system.

Static Visual Acuity

This is seeing the letters on a stationary chart. There are mixed opinions on static visual acuity and golf. When members of the pro circuit were tested, it was discovered that many were not golfing with perfect 20/20 vision. Yet many pros, particularly aging players, report improvements in their game when they update their glasses prescription. More on this in the eyeglasses chapter.

Dynamic Visual Acuity

Did you ever think about reading an eye chart that was moving? How about if you were moving? How about if you and the chart were moving? This is dynamic visual acuity. Elite baseball batters are great at this and can read the seams on the ball. This is not extremely important for golfers except when you want to follow the flight of the ball.

Eye-Hand/Eye-Foot Reaction Time

This relates to the time it takes for your eyes to respond to a stimulus and the resulting motor reaction time with the hands or the feet. As we already established, the golfer has plenty of time to make visual decisions. This skill takes on more importance in racquet sports, for example.

Speed and Span of Recognition

This is how much visual information can be processed in short periods of time like 1/10 to 1/100 of a second. In golf, this skill is not as important because golfers can take their time making decisions.

Level Three: Training These Skills

Just like body conditioning and workouts, we can train strength, flexibility, and stamina of the visual system. We train the strength and accuracy of the focusing muscle system, the eye teaming (eye alignment and coordination system) to keep the two eyes fused (working together) and turned on (not suppressing) all the time, and we train and exercise the eye-movement muscles of the eye for quicker and more accurate eye movements.

Flexibility is trained so that the focusing muscle can flex back and forth accurately and easily. Stamina of these systems is developed so the athlete can perform at peak levels for long periods of time. Do your eyes ever get tired by the end of your golf game? Just like strength or aerobic training you can train your visual system.

Sports vision training can help keep your visual system from getting fatigued. Golf requires hours of visual concentration. When you lose your concentration, you slip out of "the zone." Your putting goes downhill. You may play well for the first nine holes and watch your game deteriorate on the back nine. Training will also improve your early game if you find it takes you a while to get into the zone. Many aging golfers find it difficult to stay visually concentrated for the duration of the game. With this program, you learn ways to conserve visual energy.

Thinking Person's Profession

If golf is a thinking person's game, sports vision training is a thinking person's profession. I love to go to work every day. I find solutions for people and help create success stories. So many medical practices manage patients whose vision is getting worse. My patients do better and have more success and I enjoy that.

So enough general talk about sports vision. Let's get down to talking about and applying these new concepts to golf. In golf there is not a lot of movement going on but the game is very visual. You have to make accurate judgments with your eyes. Your eyes have to localize correctly and consistently without fatigue. Reading the greens is almost all visual judgments—telling you how hard and in what direction to hit your putt. You use your vision to stay focused and in the zone and even to pick the right clubs. So let's talk about who's doing sports vision training in Chapter 2 and then move on to my specific program for golf by analyzing your own visual system and how well yours works for you. Then I'll show you how to develop *The Pro's Edge*!

Hole In One

By the end of this chapter, you should understand:

- What sports vision training is and why it is *The Pro's Edge.*

- What the various visual skills are and how each applies specifically to your golf game.

- What this program will be able to do for you. How does training visual skills translate to strokes shaved off your score?

- How and why is golf an extremely visual sport?

Chapter

Who Does Vision Training?

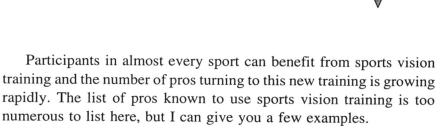

Participants in almost every sport can benefit from sports vision training and the number of pros turning to this new training is growing rapidly. The list of pros known to use sports vision training is too numerous to list here, but I can give you a few examples.

Val Skinner is one of sports vision training's success stories. It was reported in an article in *Golf Illustrated*, August 1986 by Dr. Bradley Coffey, titled "The Eyes In Golf: Seeing Isn't Believing." Val went to see Dr. Sue Lowe reporting that she was having problems placing the ball on the green accurately and felt her eyes were deceiving her. Val was having problems with her focusing and her eye alignment system so that she judged the ball to be closer and to the right of where it really was. After a treatment period of eye exercises her judgment was better than ever. In 1985, she finished in the top ten in her last six tournaments and won the last event of the year. She won the Mazda Classic in early '86. In 1994, Val Skinner was given the American Optometric Association's Sports Vision Section's Eagle Award at the LPGA Lady Keystone tournament where Val was the defending champion. In her acceptance speech she credited sports vision training for much of her success. This award is presented to a non-optometrist who significantly promotes sports vision and vision training to the public. Past recipients of this award and proponents of sports vision training are Kiki Vanderwege, Kareem Abdul Jabbar, Howard Johnson, Vince Dooly, and Lori Endicott. In 1996, the award was given to Jake Reed, a wide receiver for the Minnesota Vikings. He did a program designed to improve peripheral vision and hand-eye coordination. In 1997, it was given to Nick Faldo.

I have worked with Judy Alvarez, an LPGA pro. South Florida's CBS affiliate did a story on sports vision training and included Judy and me on it. She said about sports vision training, "I think that it's something every golfer should pursue. They spend a lot of time working on the physical aspects of the game and all the mechanics. They should spend some time working on the visual aspects of it because a lot of the time it can be very deceiving."

The fact is, as a golfer, you must master the physical mechanics of the game, but sports vision training takes you to a higher level of performance. In fact, most of the pros I work with tell me that vision training is more valuable than endless lessons in mechanics. It helps them keep a pro's edge.

An article titled "How Faldo Got His Eyes on Track," by Dr. Craig Farnsworth (*Golf Digest,* July 1996), reports that his putting problems were "optic related." In fact, he relied on his caddy to help him align his putter. Faldo found that he misaligned to the left when putts were longer than 15 feet. After his visual training he no longer relied on his caddy and three-putted only once in four rounds on Augusta's greens. I remember my father calling me to tell me that he heard an announcer on TV mention Faldo's vision training program when he took the Masters in 1996.

Other golfers who are reported to use sports vision training include: Tom Kite, Bobby Wadkins, Steve Elkington, and Ted Purdy.

I mention some of these pros because I hope that when you finish reading this book, you will be excited about doing the same program that money-earning pros use. You will dramatically improve your game with my program. It isn't difficult to do . . . most people think it is interesting and fun. You can do the program with a friend . . . or keep it a secret and watch your regular foursome turn green with envy. When your friends see your improvement, you can bet they will be wondering what your secret is. In Chapter 3, we move on to analyzing your own visual system. Pretty soon you also will have this technology at your disposal and know what the pros know.

Hole In One

This chapter gives a brief overview of who is doing sports vision training in the golf and professional sports world. The pros credit it with transforming their game. The average golfer can apply all the same techniques.

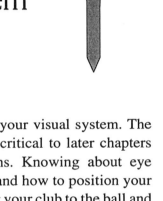

Chapter 3

Self-Test:
Your Visual System

In this chapter, we will test the areas of your visual system. The first test for eye dominance is a must. It is critical to later chapters exploring alignment and reading the greens. Knowing about eye dominance also enables you to know where and how to position your eyes over the ball. This is essential to aligning your club to the ball and target squarely and with consistency.

The other two areas in this chapter, eye alignment and suppression testing, are less critical because the strategies in this book will work no matter how you test in these areas. However, the information is useful and interesting because awareness gives you that "a-ha" feeling of revelation, letting you know what you have to work on. The information you get from these two areas will tell you how hard your eye muscles have to work to keep your eyes aligned, whether you'll tend to misjudge distances short or long, and whether your eyes play tricks on you or not. It may also explain why your eyes tire and your visual concentration wanes resulting in inconsistencies.

Eye Dominance: Are You Right- or Left-eyed?

Join the crowd. If you don't know the answer to this, you're in good company. This is the first question I ask athletes and all I usually

15

get is a blank stare. I've asked pro tennis players, pro golfers, and all-star level baseball players and I keep getting blank stares. This amazes me. These men and women have trained with the best their whole careers and this was obviously never discussed. They are doing well naturally but with sports vision training they get more of an edge.

Just as you are right- or left-handed, you are either right-or left-eyed. Just because you're right-handed doesn't mean you are right-eyed. You can be right-handed and right-eyed (same-side dominant) or right-handed and left-eyed (cross-dominant). I think this is important to know for most sports including ball sports, racquet sports, shooting, archery . . . and golf.

Your dominant eye processes information 14 to 21 milliseconds faster than the nondominant eye. You use the line of sight from your dominant eye to tell you where things are out there in your visual world, like where the ball, the target, or the hole is, or the golf ball is when you swing.

Most of the population, four out of five or 80%, is like me, same-side dominant. In other words, they are right-handed/right-eyed (or left-handed/left-eyed). The other 20% are cross-dominant (right-handed/left-eyed or left-handed/right-eyed). Knowing which you are is critical for putting consistently, reading the greens, and making square contact with the ball when you swing. So let's test for it now.

The Tests

Test One

The dominant eye tends to be the one you use when you only want to use one eye. It is usually easier to close or wink the other eye. You tend to use this eye to look through a small hole in a fence, look into a microscope, or sight a pistol. One easy test is to hold a paper-towel tube in both hands at arms length. Keep both eyes open, arms extended. Next, lift the tube in front of your eyes and sight the object far away from you. Now close one eye. If you still see the distant object in the tube, this is your dominant eye. If you don't, this is your nondominant eye.

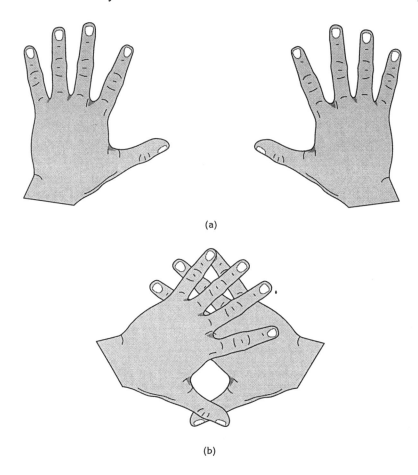

(a)

(b)

Figure 1 Eye-dominance test.

Test Two

1. Hold your arms and hands extended forward with your palms away from you. Now bring them together to form a hole with your thumbs as shown in Figure 1.

2. See which eye you use to sight an object through this hole.

3. Look at a light switch and raise hands (with hole) so that you look at the switch through the hole. Now close one eye and then the other. The eye that sees the switch (or

other suitable target) is your dominant eye. If you see the switch with both eyes make the hole smaller.

Test Three

Take a 3 x 5 index card and cut a hole in it the size of a quarter.

Look at a light switch or other target and raise the card in front of your eye so you see the switch through the hole. If you've put the hole in front of the right eye, you are right-eyed and will still see the switch if you shut your left eye. If you close the right eye, you won't see the switch and will have to move the card or your head to see it through the hole with the nondominant eye.

Cross-Dominance

It is said that cross-dominancy is an edge in golf and baseball. In golf, it is easier to keep your dominant eye on the ball as you take away the club on the backswing. You also have your dominant eye towards the cup or target when putting. Arnold Palmer, Ben Crenshaw, Tom Kite, Craig Stadler, and Jack Nicklaus are all cross-dominant.

That's not to say all the best players are. Tom Watson, Raymond Floyd, and Seve Ballesteros are not, but at some level it may have been an obstacle they overcame. More than 20% of elite pro-golfers are cross-dominant but the majority are not.

One of my neighbors, an avid golfer, came to me for an examination and we discussed his putting problems. He was not a very consistent putter. Even though he loves sports and produces bowling shows on television, he was unaware of eye dominance. He is a right-handed golfer who is left-eyed. When he widened his stance to take this dominancy factor into account, his putting instantly improved. This was because his dominant eye was now positioned over the ball properly. This improved his alignment and he was able to hit the ball squarely to the target. You will learn this secret in the chapter on alignment. For my neighbor, learning this one thing about his visual system took strokes off his game. (By the way, you also want to use your dominant eye in the viewfinder to take photos. I have patients who used to take lousy pictures until they learned they were holding the camera up to the wrong eye.)

Eye dominancy in golf affects how you should position your head and eyes in the address position for putting and is important in reading the greens. Cross-dominant and same-side dominant golfers will be doing certain things differently, in different parts of this program.

Same-Side Dominance

Same-side dominance is a plus in any target sport. In fact, studies show that a higher percentage of cross-dominance army recruits repeatedly failed on the rifle range than their same-side dominant peers. Vision training is good for target sports also. You can still be a great shot being cross-dominant if you figure out what to do with your eyes. Same-side is also good for racquet sports, bowling, shuffleboard, etc. In golf, I think the knowledge of your dominance can help with stance and putting . . . so don't feel if you are same-side dominant that you cannot be as strong a golfer as your cross-dominant peers.

Eye Alignment

If you are looking across the green at the hole and you cover one eye with your hand, does the covered eye stay perfectly aligned to the hole or does it drift in or out when it's not looking at the hole in conjunction with the other eye? The eye-alignment test answers that question and then tells you how much your alignment is off. Whether your eyes drift in and out will predict how you judge depth and location (localization). The amount of drift tells us how hard your eyes have to work to maintain eye aligment. The larger the drift, the harder your eye muscles have to work to maintain good alignment and you may fatigue before the end of a round of golf. You may also misjudge more and find it harder to concentrate. Training procedures later in the book will strengthen your eye muscles to maintain accuracy of judgments and concentration.

Problems with this system caused Val Skinner and Patty Jordan's problems with judging location of targets accurately and feeling like the hole changed location when re-looking at it.

I have one golfer who did my program and told me her eyes no longer tire when driving. Previously, on long trips, she needed to pull her car over every 30 minutes or so to rest her eyes, but now she can drive for hours. She also had difficulty finishing a round of golf, but now they stay fresh for the entire round.

This test will give us information about judgment of distances, how easily your eyes will tire, and tell you which programs to follow for your vision training workouts.

First I want you to answer a question:

Do you tend to miss shots short or long of your intended target? Now let's do the test.

Eye Alignment Test

To get a feel for this I want you to look at something about 20 feet away from you. It can be a light switch or a dot about 1 to 2 inches in diameter.

Cover your dominant eye with your hand. Now move that hand past your nose to cover the other eye. Try at different speeds until you get it.

Did the object move? If the object moved in the same direction as your hand, your eye muscles are pulling outward. If the object moved in the opposite direction, your eye muscles are pulling inward. If the object stayed still, your eye muscles are aligned straight.

Technically, we define these results as follows:

Eye muscles pulling outward = exophoria

Eye muscles pulling inward = esophoria

Eye muscles straight alignment = orthophoria

Another way to test this is to take a large serving spoon and cover one eye. Next shift it over to the other eye and see if the distant object moves. Or, you can move your hand or the large spoon back and forth from one eye to the other for about 10 seconds and watch the object move from side to side. Again, if the object goes to the right as you move the cover from over the left eye to over the right eye (with

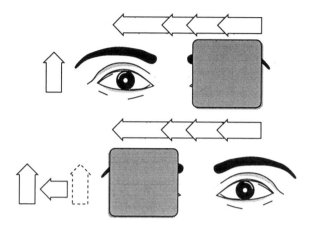

Figure 2   Muscles pull outward. If you move cover from over right eye to over left eye and object moves to the left, you are exophoric.

motion), this is exophoria. As you then move the cover from the right eye to over the left eye, the object will move to the left if you are exophoric. The opposite motion (against motion) will happen with esophoria and no motion will occur with orthophoria.

Now you should have an idea of what your particular eye alignment is like. Eye doctors who do vision training programs and measure these eye alignment findings know that eye muscle alignment affects our

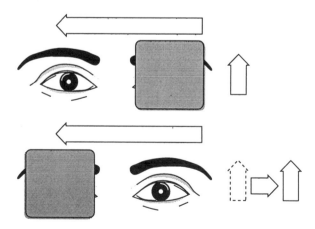

Figure 3   Muscles pull inward. If you move cover from right eye to cover left eye and object moves right, you are esophoric.

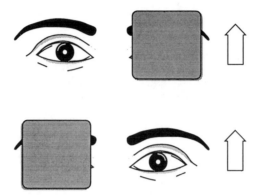

Figure 4   Eye muscle alignment is straight. If you move cover from right eye to cover left eye and there is no movement of the object, you are orthophoric.

judgment of space. The world seems farther away to exophores (eyes pulling outward) and the world seems closer to esophores (eye muscles pull in). In an intensive article in the July 1983 *Golf Digest,* Dr. Donald Teig writes of how he tested these eye alignment tendencies in the pros. "Of the 15 players whose eyes pulled inward (esophoria), 14 said their misses tended to be short. Of the 12 players whose eyes pulled outward (exophoria), 8 said their misses tended to be long."

This fits with what we know about our science. Exos judge things further away than esos. Depending on the amount of eso or exo, we can make predictions. Since the exo sees things farther away than they are, he or she may miss shots and putts long or make contact with the club face striking the ball too low. In other words, the ball may connect with the club above the sweet spot because the ball looks farther away than it really is and the club goes too far under the ball.

An eso, on the other hand, tends to miss shots and putts short and hit the top of the ball instead of hitting the ball squarely. This results in a low trajectory.

If married couples in my office are extreme opposites in eye-alignment measurements, they have comments about each other's driving. If he's a high exo, he sees the car in front of him farther than it is, while she's a high eso and sees it much closer than he does. She thinks he's tailgating, and he thinks he has plenty of room. She gets scared that he's too close all the time. He criticizes her driving that she's always too far away from the guy in front and she should hurry up.

Measuring Your Alignment

Here we're just looking for estimates and trends. Exact measurements are not critical for this book, but let's get an idea of how exo or eso you are and whether it varies or changes at different times. If your eye alignment tendencies change with fatigue or the distance you're looking at, your estimate of where the cup or target is may vary throughout your game. But don't worry—I'll show you how to accurately judge distance in spite of all this later in the book.

Let's get back to measuring your amount of exo or eso. This is done by determining how much the object moves back and forth (in inches or centimeters) and the distance you're testing yourself at. Doctors measure this in prism diopters. This is based on the metric system. A prism diopter is a movement of 1 centimeter sideways at 1 meter in front of your eyes.

To simplify this, let's work in inches. Basically, you want to measure how many inches the object you are sighting moves as you alternately cover one eye and then the other. Let's measure this at 20 feet.*

To simplify this, let's work in inches. Basically you want to judge how many inches the object you are sighting moves as you alternately cover one eye and then the other. Let's test this at twenty feet.

20-Foot Testing Distance

Inches of movement	= units exo or eso
2 ³/₄"	= 1 exo or eso
4 ³/₄"	= 2 exo or eso
7 ¹/₈"	= 3 exo or eso
9 ¹/₂"	= 4
11 ⁷/₈"	= 5

20-Foot Test Distance or Roughly Speaking

6" of movement = 2 ¹/₂ exo or eso
12" of movement = 5 ¹/₂ exo or eso
18" of movement = 7 ¹/₂ exo or eso

---

* At 10 feet, inches of movement would be halved to yield the same units of exo or eso.

If you need help judging the inches of movement, tape a 1-foot ruler over the light switch or other target you are using. Look at the target (not the ruler) but use the ruler to help you judge how much the target is moving. Again, this is not critical! We're looking for trends here.

Basically, movement of 4 to 5 inches or more or the amount of movement changing over time or with fatigue can create inconsistencies in the judgments you make in golf as to the distance and location of targets and hazards and the cup on the green. Not to worry though! You will master the strategies and techniques to overcome inconsistencies with your eye training exercises. The goal is not to eliminate your phoria but to stabilize your eye teaming system to eliminate inconsistencies in your system. We will cover this in more detail in the chapters on distance and eye exercises.

Interesting Facts About Phorias

It is not unusual to be a different amount of exo or eso at different test distances. You may even be eso in the distance while being exo in the near. In this case, you might judge the distant pin as closer than it is but a short putt as farther than it is. Test your phorias at different times. Are they always the same amount of movement or does it change (at the same distance)? If it changes on you this means you judge distances differently at different times. This causes inconsistencies.

Behavior Predictions Based On Phorias

The first time I examined my father-in-law, I amazed him. I told him that reading probably puts him to sleep. No one had ever tested him the way I did or told him this in his previous eye exams with other doctors. He wanted to know how I knew that. Well, I had measured his phoria at near (16") and it was high (9 or more exo). Whenever I examine people who are high exo at near, I have an 80% chance of being right about reading putting them to sleep. When we read, our eyes have to turn in (converge). High exos have to use a lot of energy to keep their eyes aligned when reading to overcome their drift and this is exhausting. Another interesting fact is that 90% of the kids I examine who have attention-deficit disorder (ADD) have high to extremely high exophorias. Part of the reason it's hard for them to pay visual attention and stay focused on school work is that they have to work harder to keep their eyes aligned (converged) up close for books or desk work. Their eyes function better for them looking out windows far away. It's just much easier for them to do that.

I may be slightly overgeneralizing, but for the most part one finds exos are more outgoing, less shy, good salespeople, comfortable taking up a lot of space, and more aware of what's in their peripheral vision (side vision). Their eyes want to be outward and so is their personality and even posture. There is a tendency for their feet to point outward when they sit as opposed to inward (pigeon-toed).

Esos on the other hand are generally more shy, turned inward, like their eyes. Their feet may turn in when they are sitting in a chair and their posture takes up less room. When we see esos at near, we can usually predict the person will get more nearsighted over time in their younger years, especially if they do a lot of reading, computer work, or other close work with their eyes. Just as the eye muscles want to turn in closer than what they are looking at, their vision wants to pull in from the distance and eventually they need glasses to see in the distance and their prescription needs to get stronger year after year.

Most doctors who do sports vision training also do developmental vision work which includes trying to slow down or prevent myopia (nearsighted) with special reading or computer glasses and eye exercises.

Also these phorias (exo, eso, and the amounts of it) can change throughout life. I have seen them change in times of visual stress for people like law and medical students, computer operators, athletes, and younger school children.

The vision training you will do is aimed at stabilizing your phorias and strengthening the eye alignment muscles so that your eyes will not fatigue and you will judge more accurately. When this system is not tuned up, you can have the same problem that Val Skinner had. You may start off judging distances and direction okay and as you fatigue your eye alignment muscles you may have problems in which you perceive an object or your target somewhere else than where it really is by several inches to several feet. If you work out your eye alignment muscles, you will improve visual concentration, your eyes will not fatigue, and you'll make better judgments for your shots consistently throughout the game.

Let's make a record of your own test result.

At 20 feet I am (circle one):

exo   ortho   eso

with _____ inches of movement.

A note to orthos: just because you are ortho does not mean your game cannot be improved by doing this program. You still need to build strength, flexibility, and stamina into your visual system, the same as an exo or eso. Being ortho does not guarantee accurate judgments or a strong eye-teaming system. Orthos can also fatigue early in the game, the same as esos or exos.

Eye Suppression Test

This test tells us if your brain ignores some of the information from one of your eyes. This may happen at times of stress. It is quite common, so don't worry.

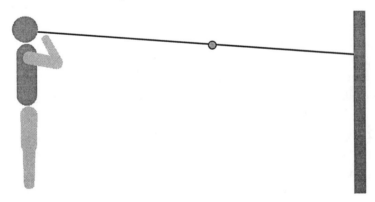

Figure 5   String test.

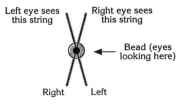

Both eyes are turned on

Figure 6   Ideal string test appearance.

All you need for this test is a piece of string 15-feet long and a bead that you can move up and down along the string. Attach one end of the string to a wall, pole, doorknob, or whatever. Hold the other end up to your nose so you can look down the length of the string.

Now I want you to look at the bead. The bead can be at 5 feet from your nose. When you look at the bead with your two eyes, I want you to notice the string with your side vision. You should see two strings forming an X-pattern (Figure 6).

When you look down the string you may not see the strings cross at the bead. The string that goes to the left as it travels away from you is seen by your left eye and the string that travels to the right as it goes away from you is seen by the right eye. Ideally, you will see what is shown in Figure 6. Therefore if you see only one string, you have an eye shutting off as in Figures 7 and 8.

Other variations of suppression can look like Figure 9.

If a string comes and goes, you still have suppression, but it may be intermittent. If you lose one string then the other at different times, you have alternating suppression. Now if you look to the end

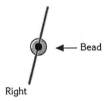

If you see the bead this way, your left eye is
shut off (suppression)

Figure 7   Left eye shutting off during string test.

If you see the bead this way, your right eye
is shut off (suppression)

Figure 8   Right eye shutting off during string test.

of the string, you should see what appears in Figure 10. If you look
at the string close to your nose you should see what appears in
Figure 11.

So you can check for suppression at different distances up and
down the string.

You also want to know if the strings cross right at the bead you are
looking at. Basically the strings do not lie. Where the strings are

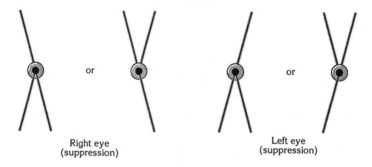

Right eye
(suppression)

Left eye
(suppression)

Figure 9   One eye shutting off during string test.

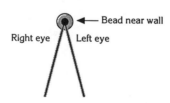

Figure 10   Looking at far end of string.

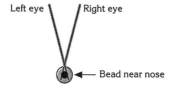

Figure 11   Looking at string close to your nose.

crossing is where your eyes are pointing. So if you are looking at the bead and you see the strings crossing farther than the bead, you think you are looking at the bead, but your eyes are actually aligned farther away (exo posture). You may misjudge objects as farther than they really are. If you are looking at the bead and your strings cross in front of it (eso posture), your eyes are really aligned closer to you than the bead. There is a mismatch between where you are "looking" and where your eyes are pointing. (See Figure 12.)

The string is a very powerful testing and training device, yet it is inexpensive. We can tie the string to a tee placed on the green at the cup and have the golfer look down the string to the cup. We can have the golfer tie the string to the tee at the address position and look down the string. I once had a golfer who usually putted short. She had an eso posture when looking down and this caused her to judge the hole closer than it really was.

Again I don't want you to be discouraged if your findings are not perfect or if you suppress. You just have more potential for improvement. Pros love me to find this stuff—then they feel there's greater potential for their game to improve. But even when we find nothing wrong, we can still train strength, flexibility, and endurance.

Figure 12 Possible string test appearance.

So again we are just gathering information. We'll work with this information later in the training chapters.

Are you excited yet?

I'm telling you, this will change your game.

Hole In One

Chapter 3 marks the real beginning of your training program. In this chapter we:

1. Explored the importance of eye dominancy to the sport of golf. How you position your dominant eye over your ball will affect your judgment.

2. Explored eye alignment and its relationship to distance judgments and eye fatigue.

3. Completed a self-test. You now know which is your dominant eye and what your eye alignment is. Are you eso? Exo? Ortho? How much?

Chapter 4

Alignment

I told my father to get his putter. I wanted to analyze his putting stance and his alignment to the target. I put a glass on the carpet about 10 feet from him and told him to line up his putter to the ball so that he was aiming right at the glass. I got down on the ground behind the putter and checked where he was aimed. He has a groove on the top of his putter that runs perpendicular to the head for this purpose.

When I sighted along this line I saw that he was actually aimed about 7 inches to the left of the glass. I told him this and he replied,

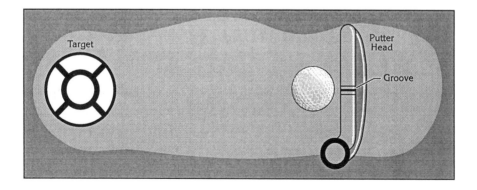

Figure 1 Putter head with groove.

"No, I'm not. I'm aiming right at the glass." I told him if he hit the ball, it would go about 6 to 7 inches to the left of the target (glass). He again insisted that he was aimed right at the cup. "OK," I said, "hit the ball and see where it goes!" He hit the putt squarely and guess what? To his amazement, it went 7 inches to the left of the glass. He was flabbergasted! He had never analyzed this part of the game. Now if he was off 7 inches at 10 feet, he would be further off on longer putts. He's probably misaligned for those short easy putts too.

So the questions are:

- Do you tend to miss most of your putts to the right or left of the cup?

- Do you miss those easy short putts?

One of the biggest problems I see with golfers is problems with alignment from the address position. Many amateur golfers (like my father) do not even realize this is affecting them and try to guess at adjustments for their putting. In the address position, golfers can have difficulties perceiving where the target is, combined with difficulty localizing properly from the address position. Many golfers are not positioned properly over the ball in the address position to aim accurately at the target.

Testing Alignment

There are gadgets on the market to aid with this from putting tracks to "laser putters." With the laser putter you align your putter at a target and then turn on the light to see if you are lined up with the target. This is a great test. Another (less expensive) option is to have a friend with a trusted eye get on the ground behind your putter and check your alignment with your target when you think you are lined up. Have your friend tell you if you're misaligned to the right or left. Try this at various distances. Even Faldo misaligned putts greater than 15 feet.

In my practice, I like solutions better than tests. If you find out you misalign to the right or left, what do you do about it? Just guess at adjustments? No! There is a way to discover and train this.

Proper Position Over The Ball

The proper position for consistent alignment in putting is to have your eyes directly over the ball, square to the line of the putt, with your dominant eye over the back tip of the ball. If you are same-side dominant, avoid having your dominant eye too far behind the ball. Now how can you tell if you are doing all of the above? Get some masking tape $1/2$- to $3/4$-inch wide and a small flat mirror. I prefer yellow tape but any color will do. In this chapter, we will use the tape for three purposes.

1. Mastering Alignment of Your Club Head

Again, we are working on putting. I feel this is where you can shave strokes off your game quickly since 40 to 50% of your game is on the putting greens and putting does not require strength, size, or quickness. Later in the chapter I will talk about alignment for the full swing and chipping.

Put a strip of masking tape on the ground or on the floor in your house. You can use a 15-foot length for now. This is "the line." Your target is at the one end and your ball is at the other. (Reminder: the cup will not always be your target as putts can break left or right, etc.)

Now place your putter face on the line so it is perpendicular to the line. The idea is to study the way that looks when perpendicular to the line that goes directly to your target and lock in on this perspective. It is said that alignment is most important for the short putts and distance is most important for long putts.

I believe proper alignment to the target is critical for any putt. Now try your pendulum swing over the line. Does your putter swing smoothly and stay square to the line? You can practice visualizing this

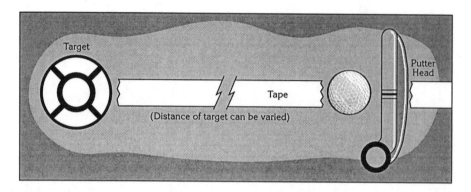

Figure 2 Proper alignment using tape.

"perspective" when the target is short or long by placing targets along the tape or using tapes of various lengths.

2. Monitoring Eye Position Over the Ball

Place a mirror down on the ball end of the tape. Make sure you are on a *flat surface* like the floor in your home. When you stand over the mirror (in the address position) and see your eyes on the line they should be directly over the line.

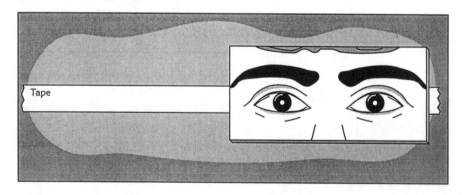

Figure 3 Eye alignment over mirror (set up for right-handed golfer).

Another variation is to run the tape over the mirror. Your eyes should be hidden by the tape. Again lock in on this perspective and practice your putting swing over this.

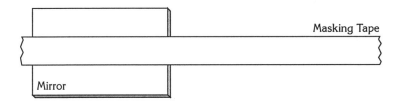

Figure 4 When eyes are hidden by the tape, you are square to the line (set up for left-handed golfer.)

It is very important for your eyes to be over the line. If your eyes are past the line, you will tend to align to the left of the target and miss to the left and if your eyes are between your feet and the line you will tend to misalign to the right. (This is for a right-handed golfer. The reverse is true for a left-handed golfer.)

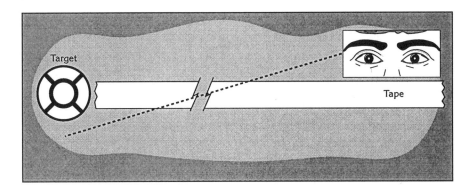

Figure 5 Eyes too far over the line project to left.

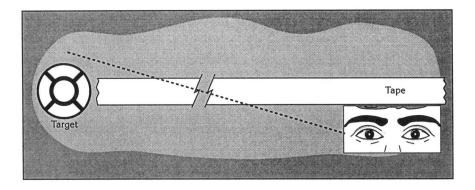

Figure 6 Eyes before line project to right.

Now you can use this set-up to help place your dominant eye over the back tip of the ball. If you are cross-dominant, you can widen your stance to do this. A friend in my neighborhood said just doing this improved his putting, but he didn't know why. I asked him if he was right- or left-eyed and he didn't know. We found out he was cross-dominant so it made sense when I told him his eyes were now positioned properly over the ball. Same-side dominant golfers have to be careful that their dominant eye is not too far behind the ball.

3. Running Your Eyes Along the Tape

Here you will simply "walk" your eyes from one end of the tape to the other and back again. Take your time—about 30 seconds to do one cycle.

a. Stand behind the ball and walk your eyes from the ball to the target and back from the target to the ball. Do this at least three times taking about 30 seconds per cycle (or 15 seconds each way) as shown in Figure 7.

b. Now repeat this from the address position. Run your eyes from the ball end to the target at the end of the tape and back again in about 30 seconds. Now this may be difficult in the beginning and you will probably feel your eyes make "jumps" along the line. This is normal in the beginning but as you practice this, they will probably disappear. (See Figure 8.)

This exercise helps in many areas:

• It improves judgment of where the target is, ensuring that your club face is accurately aligned to it.

• It improves your eye-tracking skills to aid in visualizing the path of your putt.

• It improves ability to read the greens.

• It aids in body alignment.

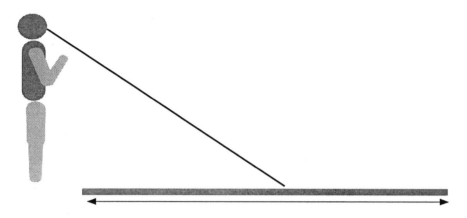

Figure 7 Variation of "running" eyes along the tape from behind the ball.

- It helps you control your eye muscles.

- It organizes your visual system by helping you appreciate visual space better.

Another variation is to run your eyes along the tape from the side as shown in Figure 9.

Remember to run your eyes up and down the tape and eliminate the jumps in your tracking.

On the golf course, start running your eyes down the greens for different ball speeds and putts.

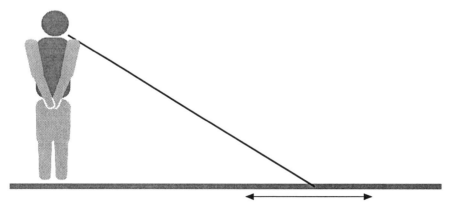

Figure 8 Variation of "running" eyes along the tape from the address position.

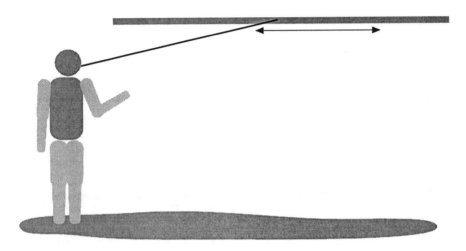

Figure 9 Variation of "running" eyes along the tape from the side

- See the correct alignment.
- Practice short putts without tape.
- Have a friend check alignment at 10 feet.
- Start to walk your eyes from the ball to the hole and visualize the break and speed of the ball.
- Align to the apex of the break (more on this later).

Other Alignment Tips

Short Putts

Alignment is most important in short putts because even if you hit the ball too hard, it will still go in the hole. There are many golf pros who advocate hitting short putts hard so that the green or the rim of the cup will not deflect the ball. In this case, the hole would be your target. (We're talking 1- to 2-foot putts).

Long Putts

Spot putting is the ability to find a spot on the green closer to the ball than the target to align with from the address position. It

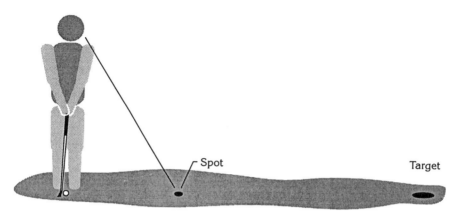

Figure 10   Spot putting technique.

is easier to align to a spot 2 to 3 feet from the ball than 30 feet from the ball.

Club Shaft Aligment

One method you can try for long putting uses your putter shaft to help with alignment and locating the spot at which you should aim.

1. Hold your putter out in front of you by the grip as shown in Figure 11.

2. Use your dominant eye to align the shaft so the ball is behind the grip end.

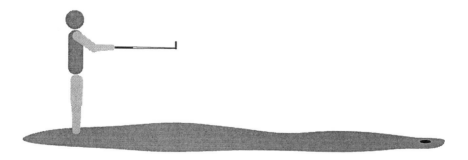

Figure 11   Club shaft alignment technique.

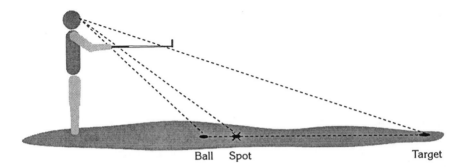

Figure 12   Visual club shaft alignment.

3. Line up the far end of the shaft with the target.

4. Find a spot 1 to 2 feet from the ball along this line to use as your "spot" target.

Using the Ball as an Alignment Tool

Another common method to use for long putts uses the ball itself.

1. Some players pick up the ball and replace it. When replacing it, they line up the letters to the spot or target as illustrated in Figure 13. Use the line of the print like an arrow or pointer when placing ball down.

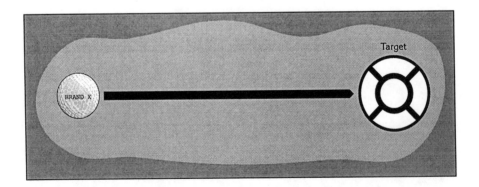

Figure 13   Using ball to align with target.

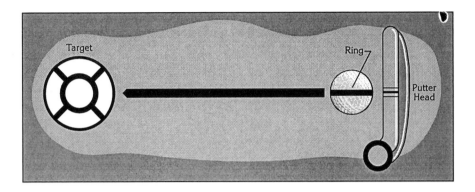

Figure 14 "Equator" method.

2. Other players draw a black line around a ball like the equator around the earth. Place the ring as shown in Figure 14. Practice stroking this ball. The goal is for it to roll, keeping the stripe steady.

Make the Target Smaller

Putting is the most precise part of the game. Instead of just stroking the ball, look at the back tip of the ball. Try drawing a black magic marker or pen dot on the back tip of the ball and using that as your alignment target instead of the whole ball, as demonstrated in Figure 15. Zoom your eyes in on the back tip of the ball.

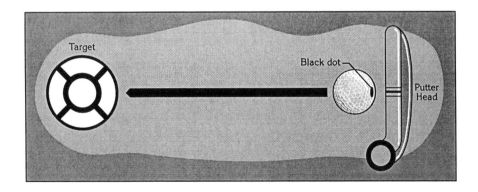

Figure 15 Black dot alignment.

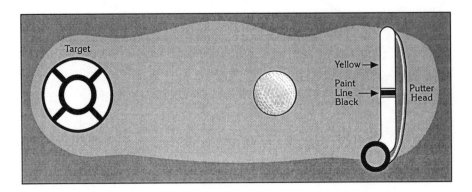

Figure 16 Painted putter.

Painted Putter

I have worked with a golf pro in my area who specializes in clinics for "handicapped" golfers. These can be stroke victims, one-armed golfers, or golfers in wheelchairs. One problem is that many of these golfers cannot place their eyes over the putter or the line. Alignment is much more difficult, so the pro instructs them to paint the top of the putter in a contrasting color as shown in Figure 16. It is much easier to see this from an angle or if you are visually handicapped.

Let's break away from putting for a bit.

Alignment for Short Chips

Remember that golf clinic I observed? I went over to see the short-chipping clinic. There the pro advocated an open stance which means his feet were not square to the line. This allows you to have a swing that is not parallel to your feet.

When he took this stance, I could tell he was not aligned with the pin. He thought he was. He hit five or six balls and each one landed 5 to 10 feet to the left of the pin. He even commented that he didn't know why they were going there.

We know why . . . he needs the tape.

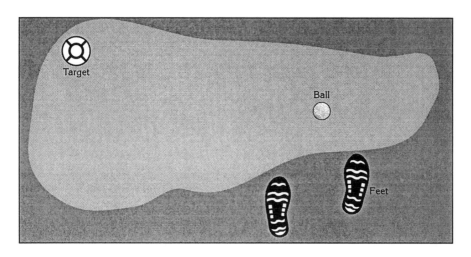

Figure 17   Open stance technique.

His perspective of where the pin was from that body position was off to the left. His eyes were misjudging. So he should put down the tape outside the green and aim to the cup.

Again study, learn, and lock into this visual perspective of being lined up with the target. Practice your swing over the tape.

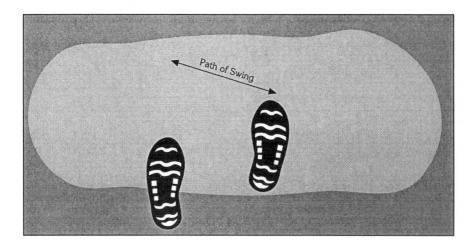

Figure 18   Open stance.

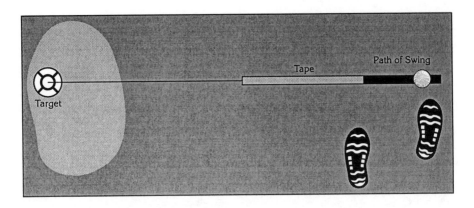

Figure 19   Tape outside the green. This should be the path of the swing.

Put down a 60-foot length of tape if you want. Or tie a rope between two stakes. The far end is the pin (flag).

The Full Swing

We'll talk about two areas here—proper alignment techniques and whether or not you block one eye on the backswing.

Alignment Techniques on Long Drives

This is the easy part. Again you can use our tapes or you can use the flag poles. Both your swing and your feet should be parallel and square to the target. Place one tape where your ball will be and one where your feet will be (see Figure 21). It is generally felt in sports vision training that you should point your eyes at the back tip (3 o'clock for right-handed golfers) of the ball for wood and iron shots. Alignment positions are demonstrated in Figures 20 and 21. Some like to find a spot along the fairway closer than their target to aid with alignment, similar to finding a spot when putting. Again you must lock in on this alignment perspective from the address position. The

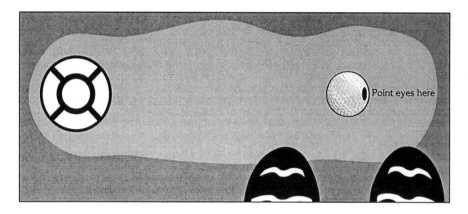

Figure 20

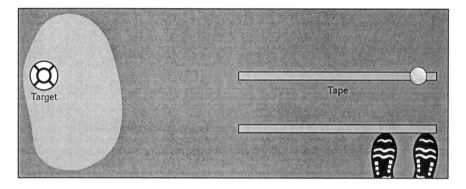

Figure 21 The ball's tape must be aligned to the target.

Peripheral Expansion Chart (p. 115) and Sticks and Straw #1 procedure (p. 65) will aid with alignment to the distant target or spot.

Where is the Ball . . . Really?

Now we'll talk about the apparent position of the ball when your club is at the top of the backswing. Where are your eyes? Are they on the ball or is only one of them on the ball (the other being blocked by your nose). The pros I've spoken to feel that your eyes should be on the ball through most of the swing.

What Happens When Your Head Comes Back with the Club on Your Swing?

What happens to me is that the ball moves about a quarter of an inch to the right. I'm right-handed, right-eyed, and exo. (Remember that stuff?) If my right eye gets covered, things move to my right. Now I can't see a golf ball move but if I put a small white dot on the floor or anything about 1/8- to 1/4-inch in diameter and turn my head to the right so that my nose blocks my right eye from seeing the dot, it goes about 1/4 inch to the right. Test this now with a small white piece of paper on the floor.

Questions

1. When you come back on your swing do you lose one eye off the ball? Come back, close one eye then the other. See if the spot disappears.

2. Does the dot or speck on the floor move to the right, left, or stay still when you do this?

3. Do you pick up more movement even if you don't block your eye but move your head? Eyeglass lenses can exaggerate this movement. We'll talk more about this in the glasses, contacts, and bifocals chapter.

So again, just be aware of this for now. Don't make yourself nuts. The last thing I want you to do is think about this in the middle of your swing during a game. But for some players it explains why they're just a little off or not getting under the ball the way they think they should be, especially when using the irons.

Try adjusting when you keep your eye on the ball to compensate for this. Do you look at the center of the top of the ball? Try adjusting your eyes to the front 1/3 of the ball or the rear 1/3 of the ball or the center of the ball when you come back. If one way improves your contact with the ball, use that strategy. Again most will do best looking at the back tip of the ball where the club will make contact. Have your pro work on your head positions.

More Eye Exercises That Aid Alignment

I have grouped together eye exercises that serve multiple purposes in the eye workout chapters of the book. Look at these chapters for additional exercises like stick in straw and peripheral expansion exercises. See pages 115 through 119.

Hole in One

This chapter explored alignment. We focused on putting and then, later, on chipping and the long game. After reading this chapter, you now know:

1. Is you club accurately aligned? We discussed expensive laser putters, but you can discover this by working with a friend and testing each other's aligment.

2. Tape and mirror techniques. Simple masking tape and a flat mirror can teach you much about your alignment.

3. Proper eye position over the ball. Do you know where your eyes are aligned? Do you know where they *should* be aligned?

4. Eye tracking exercises. We discussed a couple of simple eye tracking exercises that will help you on the greens.

5. Ball and club shaft alignment techniques. You can use both the ball and your club shaft to properly align your shots. Importantly, by practicing these techniques at home, you will be training your eyes to use these same alignment techniques on the links.

Chapter  5

Distance

I did a putting clinic at a local sporting goods store and asked the attendees to tell me the distance from the ball to the hole. I knew I had placed the ball 9 feet from the hole. Answers ranged from 7 feet to 13 feet. Nobody guessed 9 feet. The closest was a lone guess of 10 feet. Something's wrong here. This was a group of amateur golfers who were motivated enough to come to a putting clinic and look at the variance in distance judgments.

So I want you to answer the following questions:

- Do you assess the distance to the hole when you putt?

- Do you have a system to make this judgment or is it by "feel?"

- Do you "walk" your eyes from the ball to the hole to measure distance or do you just look at it?

Knowing the distance of your shot is critical to golf, especially on the greens. If these golfers were so far off on a 9-foot putt, how far would judgment be off on a 30-foot putt? They could be off by 10 feet. Now my father-in-law is pretty good with distance. He's a builder, and he constantly makes distance judgments. He's practiced at it. When he goes into a competitor's model home, he can tell how long the walls are. Golfers need to develop this type of eye training.

I feel that the goal of every putt should be to sink it in the hole. I don't care if it's a 40-foot putt. What is critical is distance and direction. To accurately set up a putt you must know the precise distance to the hole.

Three-Foot Circle Concept

Some pros advocate that on long putts your target should be a three-foot circle around the cup.

I don't like this. I think the goal is the hole. I don't like making the target larger. It just allows for more "slop" in the system. Maybe you'll miss by 7 to 10 feet. In fact, in most sports we advocate making the target smaller. In target sports, we aim for the bull's eye, not the target. In fact, I tell shooters and archers to actually zone in on and aim for the center of the bull's eye. Make the target smaller. We don't tell a baseball fielder to throw it at the first baseman, we tell him to throw it to the first baseman's glove. We tell a quarterback to throw it to the receiver's numbers. Making the visual target smaller improves

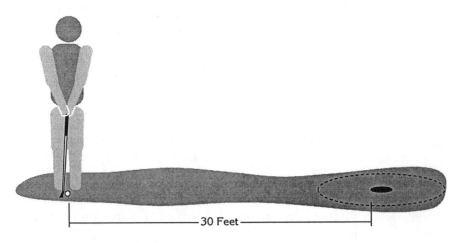

— 30 Feet —

Figure 1   Three-foot circle around the cup.

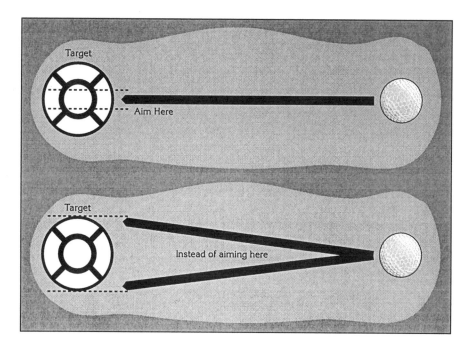

Figure 2   Aiming at the center of the cup.

precision. So, in putting, try making the target smaller. We already mentioned aiming the eyes at the back tip of the ball for certain shots. This is making the target smaller. Try making the cup smaller. Aim to the center of the cup.

Remember, distance is critical. The goal of every putt is to get it in the cup. Would it improve your score if you could one- or two-putt every green?

Test Your Judgment

Put one golf ball on the ground in front of you and roll another one 10 to 20 feet away. Now guess the distance in feet and inches. Did you walk your eyes from one ball to the other or did you just look? Now measure it. Were you long or short?

If you just look at the hole on the green you'll probably guess the distance wrong. If you're eso or exo and you just look, you may come up short or long. Also slopes tend to fool the eye. When you look up a slope this "compresses space" and we usually judge it as closer than it really is. When we're looking down a hill we'll tend to judge the same distance as longer if we just look.

Here's the Trick

Walk your eyes over the distance. This enables you to assess the distance more accurately so you can use the proper energy for the swing. Great short-game players are correspondingly great at judging distance.

Where to Start

The same tapes that we're using on the ground is where to start. Take 15-foot tape and mark off each foot. Now divide into quarters as shown in Figure 3.

Walk your eyes along the tape at a "constant pace." Start to get the feel of your eyes traveling as you monitor the distance. This will help you appreciate distance better than just looking at it. Now walk your eyes from the distance target to your feet. Now pace off this distance and get an idea of your stride. 1 step = _____ feet.

Once you've practiced this, I want you to cut tapes of 1-foot, 2-foot, 3-foot, 4-foot, 5-foot, 10-foot, and 15-foot lengths. You can go as high as 40 feet. Walk your eyes along those tapes. "Knowing"

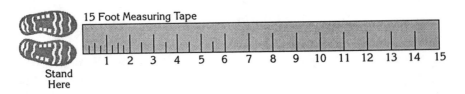

Stand
Here

Figure 3   Mark off your tape.

distance this way will help reinforce your judgment of distance. You can count off the feet in your head and lock into the rhythm of your pace.

Remember, develop a "constant" pace that you are comfortable with. It may help to hum a tune to yourself to help you with your pace by doing it to the beat.

Do It Without the Tape

1. Guess the distance of an object several feet or yards away from you by walking your eyes over the distance. Start at the object or right in front of you. Remember your pace!

2. After noting the distance in yards or feet, walk off the distance to see how accurate you were.

3. Now measure the distance. If you were off on your estimate, look at it again to appreciate the actual distance. Now re-walk your eyes over the distance at your pace several more times.

You can do this at home or in your office. Just start to use this skill to guess distances between objects. Try this when taking a walk. Guess how far that tree or mailbox is and walk it off. Guess where halfway is and check that by walking it off. Count your steps and you'll know where halfway is by dividing it in half. You can train with a friend. Each of you can guess and then see who is closer.

If you can improve your ability to judge distance more accurately, you will know how to direct your muscles more accurately. Soon your chips and putts will end up closer to the hole!

Now for the longer game, you can know what 10 yards (30 feet) is, for example, and overlap it from one point to another. This will help with longer shots and to judge the width of water hazards on the course.

In time you will not have to pace off your putts and will be able to use only your eyes to judge distance accurately.

Hitting to That Distance

Can you hit five putts on level ground from the same spot that all
stop at the same distance? We're going to eventually reference every
putt to a level and straight putt to determine our visual target on the
green. You must be able to consistently hit putts to a specified distance.
You should practice "level" putts to various distances to be able to
duplicate hitting to that distance whenever you want. Your pro can
help you with this. One way is to use a pendulum swing for putting and
come back more for longer putts. For example, come back 10 inches
for a 10-foot level putt. Come back further for longer putts and shorter
for shorter putts.

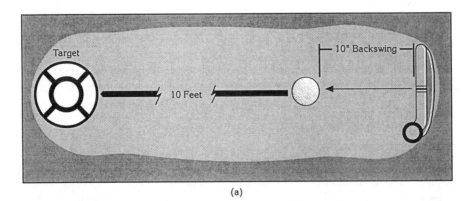

(a)

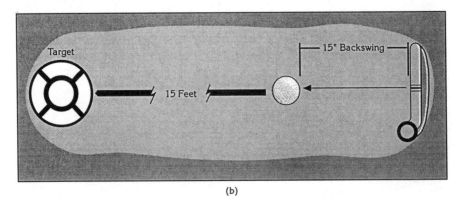

(b)

Figure 4   Pendulum swing technique.

Factoring Time into the Equation

For something to travel a distance it always takes time. So here are the questions:

- How long will it take a properly stroked level 20-foot putt to reach the hole?

- Will it take longer or shorter if the 20-foot putt is uphill?

- Will it take longer or shorter if the putt is downhill?

I want you to write down these answers on a piece of paper before you read on. Anyone I have asked these questions of has never even thought about this. I feel that when we talk about distance, we must also talk about time.

The most common answer I get to the second question is that it will take longer to go uphill. Some people tell me that the answers to the second and third questions are that it will take the same amount of time for all three putts. Of course the time of the putt may vary slightly because of conditions like longer or shorter grass or the grain. But the average level 20-foot putt hit at the proper speed to go into the hole at 20-feet is about 4.2 seconds. Now the uphill putt will take shorter time to get there about 3 seconds. The reason is that you must hit it with more force to get it up the hill and it will roll much faster and get there sooner. Conversely the downhill putt will take about 5 to 5.2 seconds as it will be hit with much less force, or gravity will pull it way past the hole if you miss.

So the next time you play or watch golf, analyze the speed of various putts. See the line and the speed of the putts. In long putts, speed is most important because speed relates to distance.

1. Learn to analyze distance and speed.

2. After making a putt, re-look at that putt.

3. Don't worry about missing putts at this point—just practice and re-look at your putts.

4. In the chapters Finding Your Visual Target and Putting It All Together you will learn how to incorporate all of this information and training into a strategy that will consistently improve your score. Have patience with this program. It all comes together!

Hole in One

In this Distance chapter, you learned:

1. A foolproof method for accurately judging distances.

2. How to judge the speed of a putt.

3. How to factor time into your putting equation.

4. How important accurate distance judgment is to your golf game.

Chapter  6

Reading the Greens

Isn't it frustrating when a friend flies in from out of town, plays on your course for the first time in his life and out-putts you? You've been practicing on those greens for years and he has never experienced them before. Well, that goes to show you that experience is not the only teacher. Your friend has better visual skills. Remember it's not strength or size or speed that counts on the greens, it's your ability to visually analyze the greens, read the breaks, and know the distance and direction to putt. Just think about the pros who fly into town and play courses they don't get to practice on.

Sight is Important

You must see clearly enough to see the breaks. In an article by Jack Runninger, O.D. in the March 1977 *Golf Digest,* "New Bifocals for Golfers," he quotes three-time U.S. Women's Open champion Susie Maxwell Berning as saying, "I never knew what they were talking about when they discussed the grain of the green until I started wearing glasses."

In the same article, Mason Rudolf stated about his new glasses, "They haven't changed my swing, but the reason I'm playing so much better with them is that the new prescription made a difference in my putting—I am able to read the greens better." In a later chapter I will go into detail about glasses, contacts, and bifocals for nearsightedness, farsightedness, astigmatism, and age-related focusing problems. It certainly pays to maintain regular visits with your eye doctor. I will also give you sources to find eye doctors who specialize in sports vision training.

Important Skills

To effectively read the green you must have great powers of observation to be able to detect subtle differences in contours and slopes. In the business, we call this training JNDs or "just noticeable differences." You want to improve your ability to detect little bumps and contours in the greens that you did not notice before. To train this, we will work on tracking skills (ability to walk your eyes over the green instead of "just looking") and we must sharpen our peripheral (side vision) skills.

Let Your Eyes Do the Walking

Stand behind the ball. Run your eyes along the ground from the ball to the cup, covering every inch along the path. Stand behind the cup. Run eyes from cup to ball. Have you ever done this before? Most amateurs I see in my practice never do this. They "just look" at the putt. One golfer that I told this to came back weeks later and told me his putting improved just from this one little tip. He had never moved his eyes from the ball to the hole or the hole to the ball along the green before. He said it instantly improved his ability to read the greens. Eventually we will work on moving the eyes along the green at the speed the ball will travel to get to the hole.

A sports newscaster in my area did a story about my practice and included an area pro named Judy Alvarez. I asked Judy if she ever tracked her eyes from the ball to the hole and she said, "yes"—to look for twigs or obstructions in the path of the putt. I asked her if she ever moved her eyes at the speed the ball would travel. She tried it and said it was much slower and harder to do this but she could see where it would benefit her.

So how many of you ever tracked your eyes along the path of the putt on the greens before you read this book? If so, did you do it at the speed the ball would travel? Again don't worry about putting this all together right now. I just want to improve tracking skills and peripheral vision to aid in reading the greens.

Eye Muscle Training

We will do eye muscle training to improve strength and control of the six extra ocular muscles. There are six muscles around each eye that move the eye. These are striated muscles which means they can be exercised and strengthened. It is usually difficult for people to move their eyes smoothly along the line. The eyes tend to make jumps along the line and you may miss valuable information. The goal is to train strength and stamina of the muscles as well as to eliminate the jumps in the tracking pattern.

Bug Walk

We will train this with a string that is 10 to 15 feet long. Secure one end to the wall or a doorknob. Hold the other end of the string up to your nose. Make sure the string is taut and that you can look back and forth along the string. You should always see two strings (an optical illusion). The one that goes to the right as it gets farther from you is the one seen by the right eye. The strings will always meet where your eyes are pointing.

Start with your eyes pointing at the string close to your nose. Slowly move your eyes away from you as if you are watching a bug crawling slowly down the string to the end at the wall or doorknob. At first the two strings should look like a "V" and as you get farther down the strings you will perceive an "X."

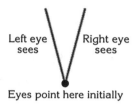

Figure 1   Bug walk exercise.

As you go down the string you may notice your eyes jump from spot to spot instead of running smoothly down the string. This is expected as there is a natural reflex to do this, but this is what you're looking to eliminate and this will come in time.

Also as you look at the string you may feel as though you are looking somewhere other than where the strings are crossing. If you are looking at the end of the string but it is crossing in front of that, you will need to relax your eyes. To do this, try to be aware of your periphery—notice the floors, walls, and ceiling out of the "corners" of your eyes. If this does not work, try looking past the wall or doorknob to relax your eyes out (diverge). Eventually your eyes will learn to point accurately. If you see the strings crossing past where you are looking you need to "tighten" up your eyes, converge more or look closer to bring the "X" closer (Figure 2).

If you see one string turn off and on your are suppressing. To eliminate this, try flicking the string a couple of times. If this does not work tap the side of your head near your eye (your temple) on the side

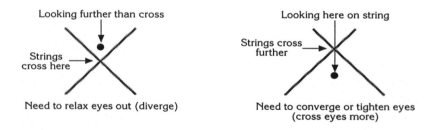

Figure 2   "X" appearance of string training.

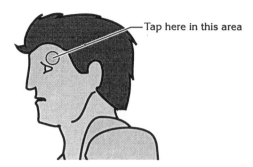
Tap here in this area

Figure 3 Tap your temple on the side that is suppressing.

that is suppressing (Figure 3). It will usually be your nondominant eye. If you see one string only and it goes to the right as it goes further from you, your right eye is on and the left eye is off (this string would go to the left) so tap the left side of your head.

Run your eyes slowly up and down the string five times per session. You should do this every day as part of this program until it is easy with no jumps. If you have trouble doing this exercise, you may have trouble using your eyes together and you should see your eye doctor.

Peripheral Training

It is important to be aware of the periphery (side vision) while you track your putts because this will make it easier to detect general slopes on the greens. While doing the string exercise (bug walk) try to maintain an awareness of your periphery. The following exercise can help train this part of your vision.

Sticks and Straw #1: Peripheral Expansion

You will need a straw and two toothpicks initially for this exercise.

1. Take a straw and draw a black line in the center of its length,

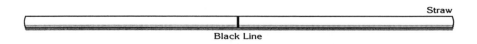

Figure 4   Draw a line down a straw.

2. Have a friend hold the straw or suspend it one to two feet in front of your nose so that you can reach it.

3. With a toothpick in each hand, try to place the toothpicks into each end of the straw at the same time without taking your eyes off of the line in the center of the straw. Try to notice the ends of the straw with your side vision first.

Again, relax your vision and be aware of the ends of the straw while you point your eyes at the center.

Variations:

1. If this exercise is too difficult at first, make the straw shorter.

2. Once you master this exercise, make the straw longer and longer by taping straws together.

3. Try to get in touch with what you are doing that let's you see way out to the sides. While pointing eyes at the center of the straw try to "see" and pay attention to the ends of the straw with your side vision.

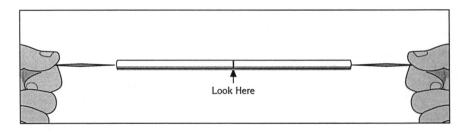

Figure 5   Sticks and straw exercise.

We will explore more on peripheral expansion in the eye workout chapter.

Using Your Putter Shaft to Read the Greens: The Plumb Bob

Most of you have heard of this. It is holding your putter shaft dangling from your fingers so that you can read the break of the greens. Many people tell me they can't do it. One reason is they try to do it with the wrong eye. You should use your dominant eye to sight this. This means that if you are cross-dominant (say right hand/left eyed), your mistake is that you may be holding the putter in the wrong hand and/or trying to use the wrong eye. If you're left-eyed, try holding the putter in your left hand for this and if you are right-eyed, hold the putter with your right hand and sight with your dominant eye.
Steps:

1. Use putter shaft held out in front of you to get a line from the ball to the hole as shown in Figure 6. Move side to side until you are on the line

2. Now dangle the club shaft vertically in front of dominant eye so that the ball is in line with the bottom of the shaft at about the clubhead.

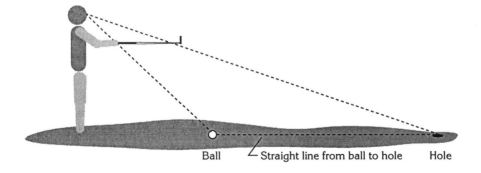

Ball   Straight line from ball to hole   Hole

Figure 6   Hold your putter shaft out in front of you.

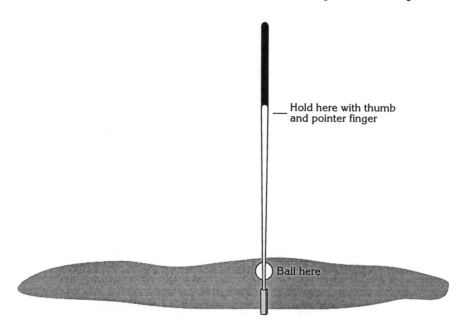

Figure 7   Vertically dangle club shaft.

Make sure shaft is vertical. This means the clubhead should be pointing toward you or preferably the cup in line with the ball and cup. If you hold it "sideways" your shaft will not be straight up and down.

This is wrong. The weight of the putter face will angle your "plumb line" and you will make mistakes. (Figure 8.)

Try to be the right distance from the ball so you can place the ball at the bottom of the shaft and see the hole closer to the top of the shaft as shown in Figures 10 and 11.

Now let's use an actual example. The green is breaking to the left and you need to aim to the right of the hole (Figure 12).

If you see what appears in Figure 13, your putt breaks to the right and you will have to aim to the left of the hole. If you have trouble with this, talk to your pro, but remember to use your dominant eye with the same-side hand and make sure the putter shaft is vertical.

Using the "plumb" is not totally scientific or reliable. It doesn't read "double breaks" or factor in green characteristics or the grain but it is still a valuable aid.

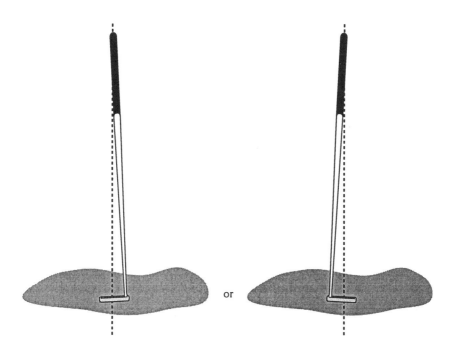

Figure 8   Incorrect ways to dangle putter. Putter head is not aligned with hole.

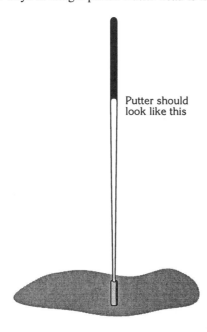

Putter should
look like this

Figure 9   Correct way to dangle putter. Head is aligned with hole.

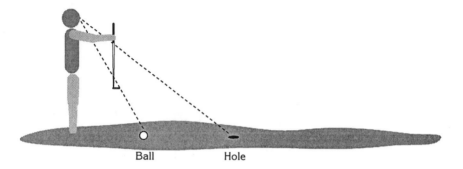

Figure 10   Correct positioning.

A Valuable Experience

You should see the greens through a pro's eyes. Take a lesson with a pro where you concentrate on reading greens. Plop a ball down on various parts of the green and on different greens. First you read the green, then have the pro tell you what he or she sees and compare

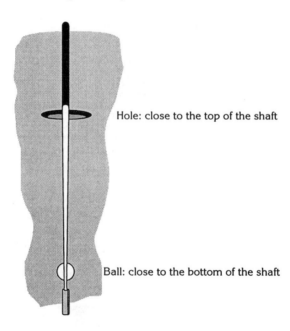

Figure 11 Ideal position of hole/club shaft. If you see this, there is no break.

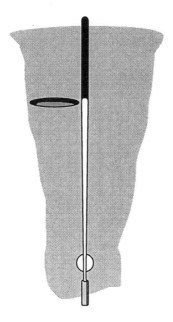

Figure 12   Ideal position of hole/club shaft. Break to the left if you see this.

Figure 13   Example of possible view. This shot will break to the right.

notes. In other words, seeing it through the "elite's eyes" will also teach you what to look for. Also have the pro work with you on the "plumb" if you have problems with it and want to master it.

Also the pro can tell you about local green characteristics. What type of grass is it? How does the grain go? Does it follow the drainage of water? In some areas the grains all go toward the ocean. In some areas the grains go toward the setting sun in the west. Bermuda grass responds to water but if flat its grain goes toward the ocean.

People who do well on the green know what to look for and "see it." Their vision is relaxed while they see everything. They do not have to get the "feel" of the greens because they are using higher visual centers in the brain to make decisions.

In the next chapter we will be using the skills we are building to assign a different "visual target" for the putt stimulus. And guess what? It will not be the hole.

Hole in One

In this chapter we concentrated on:

1. Improving your powers of observation.

2. Walking your eyes from the ball to the cup.

3. Eye muscle training for reading the greens. We used the bug walk and the sticks and straw exercises.

4. We also recognized the importance of peripheral vision when reading the greens. We discussed how, when you pull this all together, your vision should relax on the course, making this all come together for a crisper game.

5. The plumb bob. Many people complain that they can't do this. But now you know the secret—not only how to hold your club . . . but which eye and hand to use when trying the plumb bob.

6. Seeing the greens through the pro's eyes. There are many different facets to reading greens, and the "elite's eyes" can help you see what you need to be looking for when on the greens.

Chapter  7

Find a Different Target

Are all 10-footers the same? Are all 10-foot putts the same shot? No! Some are up a slope, down a slope, some will break to the right and some will break to the left. So how can the hole be the target for all of these different 10-footers? The "hole is the goal," but it is not your visual target unless it is a level 10-footer with no breaks. For other than level and straight putts, you must learn to assign a visual target that is different from the hole. If you determine the ball will break from right to left as it travels, do you have to aim your shot to the right of the hole? So why do you look at the hole before you stroke the ball? It's not what you're aligning to.

Navigation and Vectors

To understand this concept, think about navigation. Let's say you have a boat and you want to go from one island to another, and the islands are 100 miles apart. You check your compass heading and aim your boat to the far island and start traveling 10 miles per hour. Will you dock at that island 10 hours later? Probably not. Other factors will affect your speed and direction such as tailwinds or headwinds and currents that can steer you off course (even though your compass heading stays the same).

Tailwinds or headwinds can accelerate or slow your pace forward. So in perfect conditions you would travel 10 miles per hour and get to your 100-mile destination in 10 hours. Hypothetically suppose a tailwind was pushing your boat 10 miles per hour and your engines were pushing at 10 miles per hour—you would travel 20 miles in 1 hour. You might reach this island in 5 hours. Or if the wind was blowing you to the side as you traveled you would miss this island to the right or left. So if a wind is impeding forward travel 5 miles per hour you must accelerate the engines to overcome this (headwind). If there is a tailwind pushing the boat 5 miles per hour you may have to slow the boat's engines to 5 miles per hour to make it travel 10 miles distance per hour and to make it a 10-hour trip. Navigators have to factor all of this information to pick a course to get to that island at a specific time. So they do vector analysis. They pick a target different from the actual island at which to aim. They adjust for left or right drifting and adjust prop speed for an appropriate speed for the craft.

This is how you have to think about putting. If you aim your ball at the hole but the green breaks from the right to left you will miss your

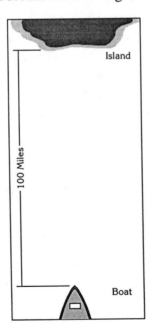

Figure 1   Hypothetical boat target.

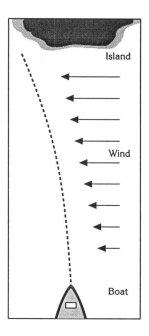

Figure 2 Boat misses target.

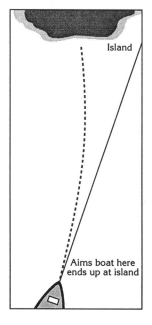

Figure 3 Navigator adjusts target.

shot to the left. If you hit an uphill 10-foot putt with the same force that you hit a 10-foot level putt your ball will not even reach the hole.

Basically, one way to think about a downhill shot is that it is like having a tailwind. The slope of the green is going to help pull the ball to the hole. You must then stroke the ball with less impact or your ball will sail way past the hole if you miss it. If your shot is up the slope you must stroke it harder to get it up the hill (like running into the wind—it's harder to get there).

Distance Adjustments

For now let's forget about putts that break to the right or left and concentrate on putts that will travel straight on level ground or up and down slopes. Our alignment will be with the hole, we just have to adjust the speed of the ball by adjusting how hard we hit the ball by choosing a different visual target.

The key is to reference it to a level putt. In other words, an uphill 10-foot putt might be referenced to a level 14-foot putt. You may have to hit that 10-footer with the impact you have mastered to hit a 14-footer that is level. Remember I told you before to practice hitting level putts to various distances consistently? This will come into play now.

Conversely a 10-foot screaming downhiller may be hit the way you would hit a 5-footer on level ground. Of course these numbers are not precise as slopes and speed of greens can vary but practice referencing your putts to level putts. Look at an up- or downhiller. Notice the different speeds that the balls travel. Watch the pros putt on TV. How many seconds does the putt last? When you putt—whether you sink it or not—reexamine your putt visually after you've made it. I always learned more in school by going over my wrong answers than from anything else. It completed the process of studying—testing and going over the answers. I hated not getting tests back at school. Just as you learn by going over tests, you learn by going over your own putts after you've putted them. Re-analyze them. Again, the hole is the goal but not necessarily your "target." Uphill putts will have a target farther than the hole and downhill putts will have a shorter target.

Right and Left Breaks

If your putt is going to break from left to right, you must adjust your visual target for alignment to the left of the hole. If your putt will break from right to left you must align with a target to the right of the hole. Do you agree? You must factor in and analyze other variables. The more the break, the more the ball will be pushed sideways as it travels and the slower the ball travels the more it will be pushed sideways. Again you've got to analyze these things over time to get good at this type of analysis.

Now most people underestimate the break. The ball is pushed farther to the side than they thought it would be. So if the green is going to push the ball from left to right, they miss to the right of the hole.

What Should You Do?

1. Read the green and determine whether this is an up- or downhill putt.

2. Read greens to tell if it will break from left to right or right to left.

3. Is the green wet or dry, fast or slow?

4. Walk your eyes from ball to hole to determine the actual distance of the putt.

5. Now track your eyes from the ball to the hole to read the breaks of the green.

6. Now track your eyes from the ball to the hole along the path you think the ball will take. "See" the ball travel at the speed it will take to get there along that path. (Remember uphill travels faster; downhill rolls much slower).

7. Determine the apex of the break. For most shots try to align in the directions of the apex of the break and not the hole.

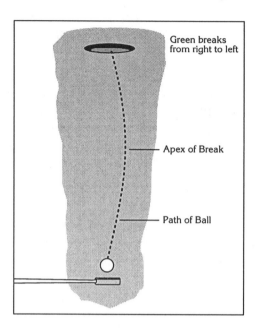

Figure 4 Apex of break.

8. Assign a new length to the putt. Add 12 to 17 inches to this length. If the ball stops rolling at exactly 10 feet on a 10-foot putt, it may roll "around" the lip of the cup instead of into it. The ball must still be rolling fast enough to roll into the cup especially if the rim is elevated.

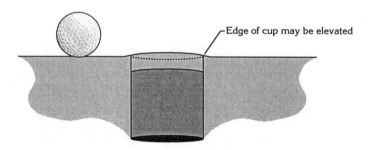

Figure 5   Take the edge of the cup into account when putting.

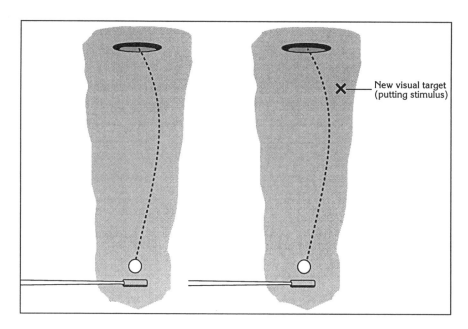

Figure 6 New visual target for example putt.

EXAMPLE

Your ball is exactly 10 feet from the cup. It is a downhill slope and the ball will roll to the left because of the break in the green. In short, you must find a new target (or bull's eye) to aim at. This target will be shorter than 10 feet and somewhere to the right of the hole.

So if you reference to a level and straight putt you might analyze that this is equivalent to a 6-foot putt aimed 20 degrees to the right of the hole. Now find your close spot along this line to align with and hit your level 6-foot stroke in that direction. Gravity and the greens will direct your ball to the hole at 10 feet.

Get it? This may be overwhelming at first. Be patient. I will go back over it in another chapter where we put everything together so

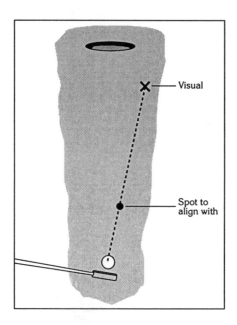

Figure 7   New line, new alignment spot.

just hang in there. Now let's go back to our example. You have walked
your eyes to get the distance, you have walked your eyes to read the
green, you have walked your eyes along the path of the putt at the
speed (and real time) the ball will take to get there. You see the ball
go into the hole. You have massaged the green with your eyes to come
up with a "target." You see the line to that target. You find a closer
"spot" along that line for alignment and you stroke the ball with the
impact of the distance of the new target.

You have referenced your putt to a straight and level putt. Use
the target as your guide for your pre-putt stimulus—not the hole.
Just align with the spot and hit with the impact of your level six-
foot putt.

EXAMPLE of a 15-foot uphill putt that will break to the right.

You analyze that the slope and the break and think it will roll
as shown in Figure 8 and 9.

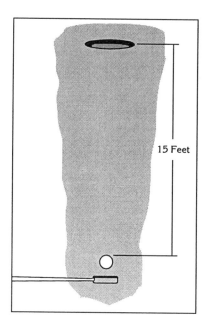

Figure 8 Fifteen-foot uphill example.

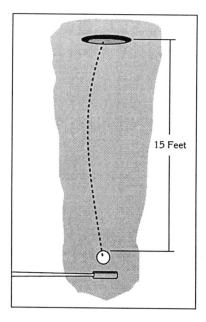

Figure 9 Analysis of where ball will go in example.

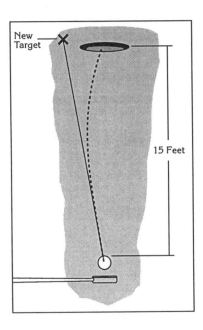

Figure 10   New assigned target.

You reference the distance to say a 20-foot level putt and because of the faster speed on the ball, the break may affect it less. You assign a new target.

Now your new visual target is 20 feet from the ball and let's say 20 degrees to the left of the hole. You massage the line for your spot—align with your spot and stroke what would be your normal 20-foot level putt aligned to your "spot" that is to the left of the hole.

Your Brain Is a Computer

The more visual information you can give your brain to make putting decisions, the better the result and consistency. Make putting a visual decision. Don't just experiment with hitting it harder or softer or getting the "feel." Twenty percent of the nerve fibers that come from your eyes go to brain centers that help muscle control systems.

Remember the following points:

1. This doesn't come quickly.

2. Re-analyze your putts after you have made them by running your eyes over the path again.

3. The faster the ball is rolling, the less it will be affected by the break. The slower the ball is rolling, the more it is affected by the break.

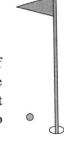

Hole in One

This chapter explored the concept of targets. Instead of aiming (as some pros instruct) for a three-foot circle around the cup, you should be making your target smaller. After reading this chapter, you should also know:

1. How to find a different visual target . . . One that is different from the hole.

2. How to reference every putt to a level putt.

3. What is your pre-putt stimulus?

Chapter  8

The Mental Game

One day an LPGA golfer came into my office all smiles. What's the big news, I asked. She told me that she had visualized every full shot and putt on the course and that an overwhelming majority of them had occurred exactly as she visualized them. She said it was like watching herself in a dream and she loved it.

So what was going on here? Pure coincidence or did this golfer create this?

In this chapter I want to talk about the mental game of golf. I have broken it down into the areas of concentration and "the zone," relaxation and visualization. I think that all these areas are interrelated.

Concentration and the Zone

What is concentration? This is the ability to focus your mind on the task you are doing. Walter Oleksy wrote in his book, *The Power of Concentration*, that concentration is an acquired habit. "Men are not born equal in their power to concentrate any more than they are born equal in their ability to play tennis or the stock market. But up to a point everyone can improve his powers of concentration in any direction."

One of the most powerful tools I feel helps in concentration is having a routine. I've even developed a routine to write this book. Every week I take notes on legal pads to organize the chapter. I visualize or think about in my head how to break it down and put it in the order I want. Usually on Sunday I sit out back of my house with a glass of water, my reading glasses, notes, and write the chapter on a legal pad. It just flows out of my head. I didn't even know I was going to talk about my writing routine until just now. The point is that my routine is working. My publisher has told me I should write on a computer. Now he says don't stop doing what you're doing. You are on a roll. I'm getting the job done. Oh, I forgot to mention that I also make sure my wife has the kids totally entertained during this time so I have no distractions while I write.

Do you have a routine when you golf? Do you get to the course early so you can relax or are you in a rush? Do you have a routine to analyze your shot, whether it's long or on the putting greens? If so write it down. Write down your routine for putting. Write down your routine for getting out of the sand. Write down your chipping routine or your long game routine. The bottom line is you need a routine that works . . . a routine you stick to.

I watched Nick Faldo on TV yesterday. He has a very definite putting routine. You may even call it a ritual. He almost always kneeled to plumb for his spot and after that he wiped the blade of the putter with his left-hand. He would then set and align the putter down with his right-hand while he touched his pant leg with his left-hand. Once aligned he would place his left-hand on the putter grip with the right and stroke.

The point is you want to develop and perfect a routine that works and stick to it!

Sample Routine for Putting

1. Analyze grain.

2. Analyze distance of putt (run your eyes over distance).

3. Track eyes to read green and plumb the hole for the break.

4. Visualize path ball will take at speed and time with eyes.

5. Find another target.

6. Find spot along that path with putter shaft.

7. Align with spot and stroke for distance of new target (referenced to level and straight putt).

You can adjust and play with this sample routine. Find what works for you.

The Zone

Everybody talks about "the zone." I was really in the zone today or I couldn't get into the zone today. When I work with athletes I always ask them what is it like when they are in the zone. Baseball players say the ball is the size of a grapefruit and it's moving slower. Tennis players say they can see the serve sooner and they see everything that's going on all over the court. Golfers tell me they just walk up to the ball and it goes where they want it. Most people have experienced "the zone," but they don't know how to put themselves into the zone. They mistakenly believe it is "luck" or it just happens. When you are in the zone, it's like you're on automatic pilot with everything just going right. But you can put yourself into that zone with practice.

Sensory Systems

In school we all learn about the five senses. Sight, hearing, taste, smell, and touch. In sports vision training we also consider balance, internal feelings such as energy level and hunger, and the little voice in our head (self-talk) or thinking.

When you're walking around in the environment you will flip from one sense to another as these senses are usually controlled by external factors. You may be watching a bird fly (visual), when someone distracts you by speaking to you (hearing). You could be set over the ball in golf and your buddies are joking around and this distracts you. You keep going in and out of different systems. You look at something, you hear something, you feel something, you smell something, etc. When this happens, the system you are using keeps changing and you are not controlling it. The key to the zone is to control which sense is dominant. For most sports you want to stay in the visual system.

To stay in the visual system, let your eyes control your muscles—not your thoughts or feelings. If we go back to our golfer in the zone, she "sees" it better. The golfer in the zone is better focused (even that is a visual word). He or she is not thinking when in the zone.

I even know a fellow in Atlanta who has the best bar-BQ around. I told him he should write a book of his recipes. He said he could not because he cooked by the smell. He added ingredients by the smell and it varied day to day with the different meats and other fresh ingredients he used. When this man cooks, he is in the zone—the olfactory (smell) zone.

To be in the zone you must control which sense you are using. For most sports you must stay in the visual. You react to visual stimulus without thinking. Like avoiding a car accident, you react reflexively and quickly to what you see without thinking. I've seen well-meaning coaches ruin a player's performance by yelling at him or her from the sidelines. The coach pulls the player out of the visual zone and into the listening zone right in the middle of a play. If the player is smart he or she will shut off the "listening" and stay in the visual zone.

You will use other systems for information in golf. For example, if you can't tell which way the wind is blowing you can tune into your auditory system by closing your eyes and turning your head until you hear the wind in both ears. When you hear the wind in both ears, your nose is pointing at the wind. This is an old sailor's trick my friend Dan taught me. Just remember to tune into the system you need for the task and you be in control of the selection—don't let the environment choose for you or you will be confused.

So when we think back to being in the zone in sports, you are most likely in the visual system. You just see it and react like a reptile. The eyes direct the motor system (muscles).

- There is no thinking in the zone.
- There is no self-talk in the zone.
- There is no cognition in the zone.
- When in the visual zone the mind is a blank.

I've had players tell me their putting improved when they stopped analyzing verbally in their heads and just walked up to the ball, looked at it, and stroked it. All the self-talk robbed them of being in the zone. If you cannot stop thinking, move your eyes from object to object without analyzing until the voice in your head stops.

Relaxation

To aid with being in the zone you should have relaxed concentration. This means you don't feel stressed, hungry, or tired. You've always got to start with the basics. Good nutrition, exercise, and proper rest are highly desired.

Mind-Body Calming Techniques

These techniques help you attain a relaxed state, reduce tension and heart rate, and help clear the mind. There are books you can buy that go into great depth about the physiology and forms. Yoga may help. Most calming techniques involve deep breathing and clearing the mind. My belief, for this program, is that if you do the following every day for 10 to 20 minutes you will be able to "call upon" this relaxed state and access it quickly when you are stressed.

Step I: Deep Breathing

Sit in a relaxing chair in a quiet place and close your eyes. Preferably use the same place each time you do this. Now take a deep breath while counting to four in your head and exhale while counting to four (each count = 1 second).

In 2, 3, 4

Out 2, 3, 4

Do this ten times and see how relaxed you are. Hopefully your mind was clearer when you were counting the beats. Another variation is:

In 2, 3, 4

Hold 2, 3, 4

Out 2, 3, 4

Concentrate on taking the breath in at your lower stomach and pulling it up through your chest as if you were filling a balloon from the bottom up. This actually allows your stomach to go in and out, not your chest. This also allows the breathing to be deeper. Focus on counting the breathing and keeping the mind clear. Eventually you could do this to classical music with the same beat. Think about breathing in relaxation and breathing out tension, increasing your concentration with each breath.

Longer Version

Start with the previous routine and after 10 cycles, picture an "O" in your mind. Stop counting and just see the "O." You can make it larger, smaller, change color, etc. If thoughts enter your mind, just cancel them and replace them with the "O." Make multiple "O"s or "O"s within "O"s. Just clear your mind of any other thoughts or pictures. Let your breathing slow down and get shallower and shallower. Allow yourself to establish a comfortable rhythm. When you feel very calm and relaxed, open your eyes slowly. If you do this consistently, you will be able to access this state within minutes when you are stressed.

I remember one time in school I looked at a neuroanatomy test and felt panicked. The questions seemed like they were in a foreign language and I could feel my adrenaline flowing and I was stressed. Since I had learned this relaxation technique I turned the paper over, closed my eyes and did the breathing with the "O" for about two minutes. I opened my eyes, felt relaxed, and did fine on the test.

One Last Variation

After you start breathing, systematically tighten and relax all the muscles in your body. Start with your toes—tighten for two to three breaths and relax for two to three breaths. Then your calves for two to three breaths; then your thighs, back of your legs, buttocks, stomach, chest, fists, forearms, biceps, triceps, shoulders, neck, and face. Tighten, hold, and release each body part and the result should be the release of tension substituted by a state of greater relaxation and calm.

The idea is to be able to relax and clear your mind so you can be in the "present time zone." This means you are not upset by that last bad putt or swing. Stay in the present time zone! Don't look back.

Try this. Do this anywhere you want. Observe something in your surrounding. Just look—do not analyze. Notice the color, shape, or the distance between the object and other things. How far is it from you? If other thoughts appear, disregard them and see how quickly you can get back to just seeing. Try to notice things in your surroundings that you never noticed before. Trace objects with your eyes. Your goal is to stay in the visual zone for longer periods without being distracted. This will improve your concentration, relax you, and clear your mind of worries, . . . and help you access the zone.

Saving Visual Energy

Another important concept of sports vision training is to conserve visual energy so your eyes don't tire near the end of the round. One client I knew told me he could hardly keep his eyes working on the last few holes. I told him to rest his eyes by looking at the horizon instead of following his opponents' swings, balls, etc. with his eyes. Or just look at the ground and save energy. Eye exercises will increase visual stamina, but you must also conserve energy as you go.

Positive Affirmations

You can plug in positive affirmations to your breathing exercises by saying to yourself

I – will – putt – well

I – will – putt – well

instead of

In 2, 3, 4

Out 2, 3, 4

There is just one important warning. Never use a negative in an affirmation. The subconscious does not register negatives. The affirmation should never contain "not" or "never" type words. You should never say I will not miss this putt in your affirmations. The subconscious hears "I will miss." You should say in your head—I will putt well or I will get it in the hole. These are positive affirmations. In fact, my wife (a counselor) told me when our children were very young not to use negatives when you need to get their attention. If you see a child going into the street do not yell, "Don't go in the street!" The child's subconscious will hear "go in the street" and be confused. Instead yell "stay on the grass" or "stay on the sidewalk." These are positive commands and are better understood. So the bottom line is train with positive affirmations.

Visualization

What Is Visualization?

Visualization is the ability to form mental pictures in your mind or in other words, your "mind's eye." You can recall past experiences (visual memory) or use your mind's eye to create visual pictures of synthesized events (visual construct). You can visualize at the scene or away from the scene. A builder can look at a lot and visualize what kind of house would look good there or she can sit in her office and close her eyes and visualize it there.

There are several studies that show that you can develop abilities just as well by visualizing performance as by actual practice. In fact, your brain doesn't know the difference between visualization and the real thing. Visualizations can be a big factor in developing a consistent swing. Twenty percent of the visual fibers leaving each eye go to areas that control your muscles and movement.

We have already introduced visualization techniques in previous chapters. You are already rehearsing in your mind what you are going to do when you track your eyes from the ball to the hole in putting. We are doing tracking exercises with the tape and string. In putting you must see in your mind's eye the:

1. Speed and direction of the putt (the path).

2. That the ball ends up in the hole (you must complete the visualization).

3. The target as your guide (not the hole).

4. NO NEGATIVE IMAGES (like visualizing a miss).

Another key to visualizing golf is you must see a target. We spoke of this in the putting area but not in the longer shots. Even with the woods and long irons you should see where the ball will land as a target. You should analyze this area with your eyes to predict how the ball will roll once it hits. So for your long game and chips you:

1. Must have a target.

2. Must see the trajectory of the ball.

3. Must see where the ball will land.

4. Must see what the perfect shot will look like in your mind.

Very importantly, *don't use your muscles in your visualization*—just your mind. Spend 1/10th of the time visualizing your swing in your head as you do on the driving range and that time will be well worth it.

You can also rehearse playing a course in your head. One pro walks the entire course without playing it to gather visual information. He takes a notebook and makes notes about every hole. That night he plays the entire course in his head. He picks his target for every fairway and sees himself hitting his target on every shot. He feels this is more valuable than actually playing the course. Try walking a hole or an entire course just to visualize how you would play it.

More Tips on Visualization

1. As difficult as it is to visualize in our heads, it is more difficult to actually watch ourselves from afar in an "out of body" visualization. This is also thought of as being a participant observer to our own activity. However, many elite athletes can do this.

2. When practicing, don't look at your performance as good or bad, just re-do certain shots but first re-visualize.

3. Replay good plays back in your head.

4. To be a good visualizer you should be a good observer and have good visual skills.

5. In golf there is a lot of time to drift mentally—remember to stay in the visual.

Before we move to some techniques there is one more very interesting fact to know about visual thinking. When most people think about something visual in the past—something that has already happened that they have seen—their eyes move up and to their left. When you are trying to construct something visually in your mind you will usually look up and to the right. Police interrogators use this to help judge if a suspect is telling what he actually saw (eyes up and to his left) versus something he is constructing or making up (eyes go up and to his right). Negotiators also use this to read the other person.

Now, close your eyes:

1. Look up and to the left and recall everything about a good past performance.

2. Look up and to the right to visualize a future positive experience you will create.

See if this works for you.

Visualization Procedures

The best place to start becoming a better visualizer is to become a better observer. Find something in your environment to study. Look at something with plenty of detail such as a painting, vase, or bowl of fruit. Look at every detail with your eyes. Run your eyes over every nook and cranny of the object. Trace edges with your eyes. Notice every swirl, size, color. No self-talk here—just look and observe by tracing your eyes over it. Stay in present time. This procedure will improve concentration, visual memory, and observation skills. Now close your eyes and see if you can remember every detail. Do this three to five times a week.

Closed-eye Visualization

There are many variations of these procedures. Can you visualize a scene in your head?

Close your eyes and see the front of your house. Can you see it? Can you see the door, the windows, garage, trees, and shrubs, etc? Create the details and then try to create the panorama view of the entirety. Now zoom in and out to each detail like windows, doors, trim, etc. See it in color. You get the idea. Practice this with other scenes.

What If I Can't See Anything?

Some people claim they cannot see anything in their head. They just see black. We try to develop visualizations by doing the following.

Just close your eyes and see black for 5 minutes. No self-talk, just be there. After looking at black for 1 to 2 minutes, you will begin to see some flashes of light or light spots. Just keep watching. Don't think. Do this daily for 5 minutes. Once you see light, try to visualize simple things like a circle, square, or triangle. Then change color and size. If this is too difficult, look at yourself or a scene in the mirror. Close your eyes and see if you can keep it in your head.

What Is All This For?

In golf, you want to be relaxed and have a clear picture of what you're going to do before you do it. You can use these skills for pre-round rehearsal. Your visualizations skills will help you be a better observer to read the greens and visualize the path and speed of your putts better. Your longer game will improve if you visualize your swing and have a target for each shot and visualize the ball's trajectory. This will improve consistency. If you must constantly "get the feel" or "get up" for the game, you are in the muscle memory system. Your "feel" will change from green to green and you will not be consistent. *Stay in the visual system and you will stay in the zone.*

Hole in One

In the mental game, several factors are important:

- Develop a routine.
- Learn how to place yourself in the zone. Practice this so you can do it at will.
- Learn what is involved when you truly concentrate.
- Practice relaxation and mind-body calming techniques.
- Practice visualization.
- Stay in the visual system.

Chapter 9

Glasses, Contacts, Bifocals and Golf

In previous chapters, I mentioned some golfers who claim that wearing glasses improved their game and helped them read the greens and the grain on the greens. Why do people wear glasses? To see better. For most people seeing better allows them to function better. I will tell a story later though about a friend who has a pair of glasses that he sees well out of but that warp or curve straight surfaces. He cannot play golf in that prescription even though it makes the chart clearest of all his glasses.

Most people wear glasses because they are either nearsighted, farsighted, have astigmatism in addition to that and/or are presbyopic—which means the lens in the eye does not focus like it used to and they need a separate reading prescription or bifocals (Figure 1). Bifocals are lenses that have different powers in the same lens to be used at different distances. More on this when we talk about lenses.

Why People Need Glasses

"Nearsightedness" is exactly what is says. Without glasses these individuals see better up close (near) than far—thus nearsighted or

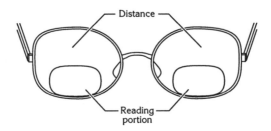

Figure 1   Bifocal lenses.

sighted at near and blurry at distance."Farsightedness" is the opposite. It is easier to use the eyes in the distance than up close, although many of these people see clearly without glasses when they are younger. They just focus the lens in the eye closer than what they are looking at to make it clear. When they are younger it is easier to do and may not affect them although many children with reading difficulty may be farsighted. When they read a book at, say 16 inches, their eye focusing muscle works like it is at say 8 inches. They can do it and make the print clear but it exhausts their system and is harder to stay focused. School screenings usually miss these kids because they can see 20/20—they're just using excessive energy to do it. They may have to focus their eyes like they are reading a book to make the 20-foot chart clear. It's like walking in 10-pound shoes.

"Astigmatism" further compounds near- or farsightedness. Probably eight out of ten people with glasses also have astigmatism but they don't know exactly what it is. It means that you need a different Rx (prescription) for one directions of line versus a line 90 degrees away. The lens in the glasses then would have a different Rx, for example, from 3 to 9 o'clock than it does from 12 to 6 o'clock. As you rotate this lens you change the "axis." In other words if a person with astigmatism looks at a plus sign without their glasses the horizontal

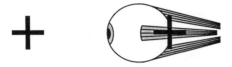

Figure 2   Plus focuses on back of eye. No need for glasses.

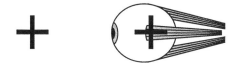

Figure 3   Nearsighted — plus sign lands short of back of eye.

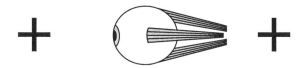

Figure 4   Farsighted — plus sign focuses farther than back of eye.

and vertical parts of the plus will focus at different locations after it goes through the front of the eyes. (Figure 5.)

"Presbyopia"—most people mistakenly refer to this as farsightedness—is a condition where, as the eye ages, it loses the ability to focus up close. I am 45 now and cannot read without reading glasses, even though I see 20/20 in the distance. People who wear glasses to see in the distance eventually cannot see to read through them and need bifocals or two separate pairs. Some nearsighted people

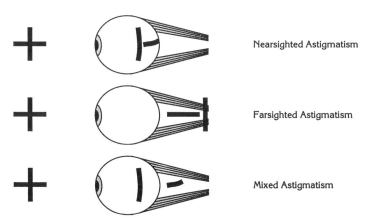

Figure 5   Three variations of astigmatism. Horizontal and vertical lines focus at different distances from each other.

can just take off their driving glasses to see up close. So again presbyopia is not farsightedness. Instead it is when the eye's focusing system stops being able to change the shape of the lens inside the eye that used to focus to a closer distance.

The Eye Chart

This measures your visual acuity. For example, if you can see the letters that are 8.8 millimeters high from 20 feet, you are 20/20. If the letters you can see have to be twice as big—17.6 mm you are 20/40. If the letters have to be 10 times larger, 88 mm (or 8.8 centimeters) for you to see them from 20 feet you are 20/200. It's seeing a certain size at a certain distance. Most people wear glasses or contact lenses to see 20/20.

Characteristics of Lenses

I consider myself fortunate to have the experience of grinding lenses and making glasses in my youth. My father was an optician and so was I before I went to optometry school. He sent me to train in a wholesale lab where we ground lenses and assembled glasses all day. I also learned a lot about how to solve problems that people had with glasses in his office.

Basically lenses bend the light so that it focuses on the right part of the back of the eye (retina) so that you see clearly.

Nearsighted lenses are concave lenses (thinner in center) and move the image from in front of the retina onto the retina. They can do some funny things. They make the world smaller. The stronger the lens and the farther from the eye it sits, the smaller the world. If you're nearsighted try this with your glasses. Lift them up and down in front of your eyes and see if you can see things change size. Move them forward away from your eyes and watch things get smaller. They also "flatten" your world and narrow your view because of distortions in the periphery or edges of the lens. This is why nearsighted people love

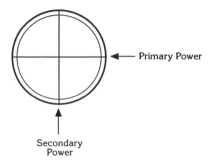

Figure 6   Lens for astigmatism glasses.

contact lenses. They make the world larger (or maybe the right size), don't distort on the edges (you're always looking through the center), and allow for much better peripheral vision.

Farsighted lenses are convex lenses (fatter in center) and tend to magnify the world. Some farsighted people are not happy in contacts because they make the world smaller than the glasses but I find that most farsighted people are still happy with contacts.

Astigmatism lenses have different prescription in the same lens 90 degrees apart. If you turn the lens in front of the eye it will distort things so the glasses must be kept at the proper axis.

Soft astigmatic contact lenses must be made so they cannot rotate or spin on the eye or vision gets blurry.

I have one patient who has an astigmatism. When I give him glasses that make the chart the clearest, they put a curve on straight edges. To keep edges straight I have to weaken his Rx slightly. He wears the weaker Rx for golf because he can't make accurate judgments through the stronger ones even though he sees better with them. I have to be careful when I have pros change their eyeglass prescriptions in the middle of their season. It may throw off their game until they get used to it.

More on Contacts

You may see 20/20 on the eye chart with several different brands of contacts. However if contrast sensitivity testing is done through these brands and you score better on this test with one particular brand, you may perform a little better through this brand. You may read the greens better and see the grain better. Ask your doctor if he or she has a contrast sensitivity chart and is willing to try a few different brands.

Prescribing Is an Art as Well as a Science

Not all prescriptions are the same—not all lenses are the same. My father always wondered why a customer would come into his office with three different prescriptions from three different eye doctors that had examined the patient's eyes within a one-week period of time. He thought they should all be the same. I can have three people with the same prescription "measurements" get different prescriptions from me based on how they respond to the prescription and how they want to use their glasses. You may want to look up a sports vision doctor in your area to help you decide on what Rx to use for golf.

All Lenses Are Not the Same

Rx lenses are made by having the curve of the front of the lens differ from the curve of the back. You can make the same prescription out of lenses with different front curves as long as you adjust the grinding of the back curve of the lens. The curve of the front of the lenses is called the base curve. I have seen patients unable to wear glasses comfortably, even though the Rx is correct, because of the base curve of the lens. Sometimes all that is wrong with a pair of glasses is that they're made with a base curve the patient is not comfortable with.

Bifocals with Golf

I suggest to most golfers that they do not wear bifocals. The bifocal (or progressive) portion of the lens is set to focus at about 16 inches

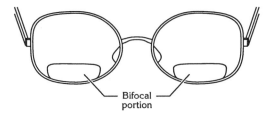

Figure 7   Bifocal set slightly lower.

and blurs the ball at the address position. If the bifocal has a line, it also gets in the way and causes shifts in head posture to look around it. Most players should get a pair of glasses without a bifocal for golf! But if you need them, have your eyecare professional design one of two different things:

1. Bifocals that are set so low in the frame that they don't interfere with your game. When you want to see the scorecard or menu later, you lift them up or tilt your head way back to get into that area of the lens.

2. Place a small bifocal in one lens only out of the way of your golf game. If you need to see the scorecard or menu, look to the side (away from your game) and read it.

Again if you find a sports vision expert, he or she will know how to do this. Just getting rid of your bifocal may help your game.

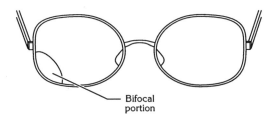

Figure 8   Bifocal option appropriate for right-handed golfer.

Exceptions to the Rule

As people age, they may have problems even focusing 5 feet in front of their eyes. I have one patient who complained that he could not see the ball at the address position clearly out of his glasses. We solved that with a bifocal designed where the bifocal was set to see well at a distance of 5 feet instead of 16 inches for reading. Again a good eye doctor should know how to adjust the prescription to do this. My patient cannot read through these "bifocals" but the ball is now clear and he's back in the game.

Sunglasses and Golf

If your eyes feel dry and irritated when you play golf, you should wear sunglasses. There are eye health reasons why you should wear sunglasses. The sun gives off ultraviolet rays that cause skin cancer around the eye, cataracts, and damage to the retina. Infrared is also given off that causes heat and damage to eye tissues.

Not All Sunglasses Are Created Equal

Not all sunglasses block these rays effectively. Labels can be misleading. If it says "Blocks UV," that isn't enough information. It must say "UV 400," or "Blocks UVA, UVB, and UVC." Again, ask an eyecare professional which brands are the best. Also beware of distortions and imperfections in lenses. Get lenses that have been ground and polished.

Sunglasses should:

1. Block UV and infrared.

2. Be ground and polished with no distortion.

3. Be easy on the eyes. Try smoke, green, or brown lenses.

4. Be large enough but not block periphery.

5. Be a safe impact-resistant lens.

Photochromatic Lenses

These are lenses that get darker in the sun and lighter inside. These are ideal for golfers when lighting conditions change. For example you may play through the afternoon and as the sun goes down or if it gets overcast these lenses will lighten when regular sunglasses might be too dark and yet still block all of the UV.

In the past, some people were not happy with these lenses as they did not get dark enough. They were also temperature sensitive. They would not get as dark in the heat as in the cold. The lens has recently been improved and now works fine. If you haven't tried the new one— give it a try. Have your eyecare provider show you a sample.

Remember that most of the information furnished to the brain to make your shots comes from the eyes. So take care of them. Later I will tell you where to look for experts in sports vision.

Hole in One

This chapter explained:

1. Why you need glasses.

2. Characteristics of lenses and how they may affect your golf game.

3. Why you should not wear bifocals as a golfer— unless you work with an eye doctor who can tailor a bifocal to your game.

4. How contact lenses affect your vision and game.

5. The importance of wearing sunglasses when playing golf.

Chapter 10

Eye Workouts and Programming

This chapter expands on some vision training exercises you may want to add to further strengthen and maintain the visual skills you have already developed in previous chapters. These are procedures you can try at home with common household items that are portable. In the office, we use much more sophisticated instruments and "gizmos." There's nothing as effective as a vision training program in the doctor's office, but these procedures are very effective. These procedures should come with practice if you have a fairly normal and healthy visual system. Hopefully you have your eyes examined regularly. If not, get them examined. Besides making sure your eyes are working properly together, it is important to routinely rule out eye diseases that cause blindness yet are easily treated if caught early enough.

If you have problems with the string procedures I outline below, discontinue them. You may have eye teaming problems and should then see an eye doctor who specializes in this specific problem.

The String

I am working with an LPGA touring pro right now who is having problems when putting. She says that when she looks at the cup, looks away, then looks back, it moves to another position on her. She also says that when she tries to track her eyes from the ball to the cup her eyes "explode." She is high eso (over 9 units) and cannot do the bug walk on the string out past a few feet from her nose—her eyes just won't diverge enough. She is fine with the tape on the ground but cannot do the string. The bug walk is a difficult procedure so we had to make it less difficult for her and I may eventually drop the string from her workout for now. So if you are having trouble with the bug walk try these other procedures first. If you continue having problems, go to a sports vision doctor.

One Bead on a String

1. Place one bead on a piece of string about 8 to 10 feet long.

2. Mount on wall or door knob and hold end to bridge of nose. Do you see two strings? Do they cross at the bead?

If you don't see two strings, do anti-suppression techniques mentioned before like tapping the side of head and opening up your awareness of your side vision (see pages 65 and 66). Remember the string that goes to the right as it travels from you represents your right eye.

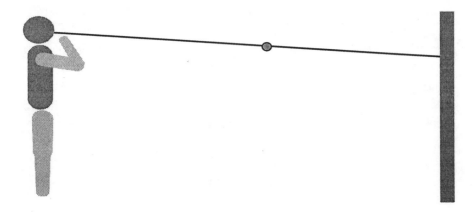

Figure 1   One bead on a string exercise.

If the strings do not cross at the bead, but instead in front of it (eso), you have to relax your eyes out and be aware of the periphery. If you see the strings cross past the bead, you must tighten your eyes and converge closer. The goal is to see two strings that cross at the bead.

Three Beads on a String

Once you can do one bead on string, add two more beads.

1. First look at the closest bead, see the strings cross at the bead.

2. Next look at the middle bead, see the strings cross at the middle bead.

3. Next look at the far bead, see the strings cross at the far bead.

4. Come back to the middle bead.

5. Back to the near bead.

6. Back to the middle.

7. End by going back to the distant bead and relax.

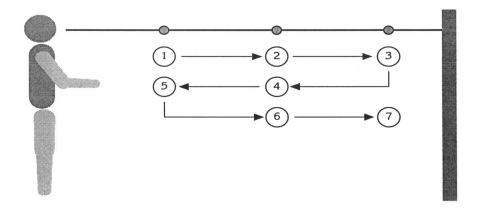

Figure 2   Three beads on a string technique.

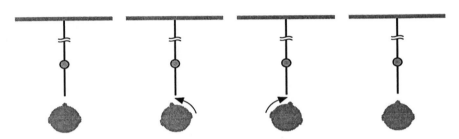

Figure 3   Variation of bead on string technique.

Variations

You can vary the time you spend looking at the bead. Hold on each bead for 5 seconds on one set, look at each bead for 10 seconds on another set and do each bead for one second. Now to build additional fusion flexibility:

1. Look at bead 1 and turn your head to the left and right a couple of inches and then back to center.

2. Look to bead 2 and rotate, etc. through the process.

3. Now look at next bead and do same. Go through one set doing this.

Bug Walk

Now go back to the bug walk. Try to build up to five sets per workout. It may help in the beginning to have a friend move a bead up and down the string like a bug. Remember, a set on a bug walk would be:

1. Start on string close to nose and walk eyes out to distant end of string.

2. Walk eyes back from distant end of string back to nose.

3. Walk eyes back out to end and relax.

(This is one set).

If the above does not come together for you or you feel your performance decline over the first two weeks, discontinue. See your eye doctor for guidance on this procedure.

Peripheral Expansion Chart

Improving your peripheral vision abilities will help with alignment and reading the greens and the slopes of the course in general. Use the chart shown in Figure 4.

1. Hold chart at eye level.

2. Do not take your eyes off of the heart in the middle.

3. Try to see the first 4 letters out with your side vision (see Figure 5).

4. Now widen your vision and concentrate on the next four (see Figure 6).

5. Now to the next four, etc.

The goal is to be able to manipulate your side vision out to the farthest set of letters. Feel what you're doing with your eyes to do this.

Variations

Try this with one eye at a time and then both eyes together. Once you've mastered this, make the chart larger on a copy machine. Do for 3 minutes per workout.

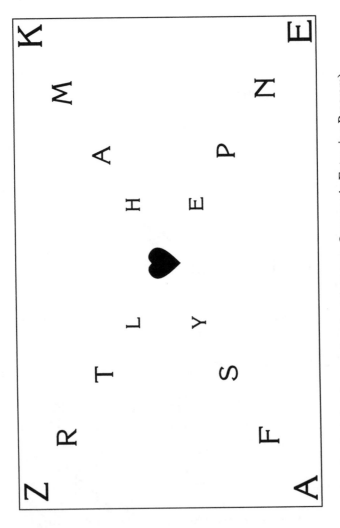

Figure 4 Peripheral expansion chart (courtesy Optometric Extension Program).

Figure 5 Eye chart, next level.

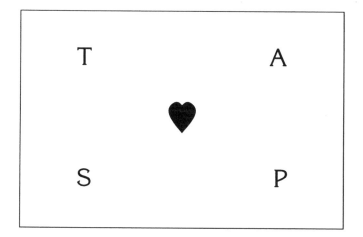

Figure 6 Eye chart, next level.

Coin Toss

Initially this activity seems too simple to be valuable but you can incorporate so many areas of this book into it. It is also something you can do inside on a rainy day.

1. Place container on ground. You can use jars or bowls of various diameters.

2. Toss coins into container. Now this sounds simple but here's what I want you to do.

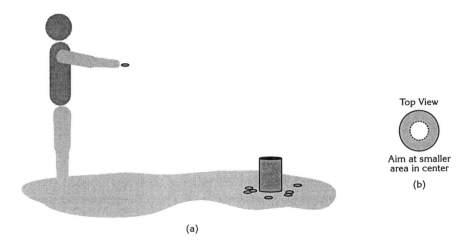

Figure 7   Coin toss exercise.

a. Get a container with a 4-inch opening. Toss 50 pennies into container a few feet away. See how many you get in.

b. Now make target smaller. Instead of aiming for the container aim for the center.

Does this improve your accuracy? Did you get more in?

c. Now visualize the trajectory of the toss before you shoot. See the penny go into the container (complete your visualization). Does visualizing the shot and making the target smaller improve accuracy?

Variation

Work on this with different sized containers at different distances. Also try different trajectories. Try with right eye only, left eye only, both eyes together. This will program your brain (like a computer) to use more visual information for golf.

Sticks in Straw #2: Localization

This activity improves your ability to localize objects at the same point in space with each eye. You need a straw and a toothpick.

1. Your assistant holds a straw about 18 inches in front of you.

2. You look at one end of straw and try to put the toothpick into the end of the straw. Try to do this with your eyes— not by feeling around the edges of the straw. If you miss pull your hand back and start again.

3. When successful, your assistant should move the straw to another location—vary height and angle of straw. Hold head still and use eyes.

4. If too difficult use a paper towel tube and your finger. Then go to an unsharpened pencil and slowly increase difficulty until you can do a toothpick into the straw. Do this with the right eye, left eye, and then both eyes together. Do this four minutes per workout.

Four-Corner Fixations

This will help with eye movement skills, visualization skills, and peripheral expansion.

1. Find a wall that has four corners not blocked from view.

2. Label corners 1, 2, 3 and 4 visualize the numbers being there (Figure 8).

3. While looking at corner 1 try to see out to corner 2 with your side vision then move eyes to corner 2 trying to do it in one accurate eye movement.

Figure 8   Visualize four corners.

4. Now try to see corner 3 and repeat.

5. Now see corner 4 and try to repeat.

6. Now back to corner 1.

7. Repeat procedure going now counterclockwise 1 to 4 to 3 to 2 to 1.

Variations

Attempt this at a constant pace and try increasing your pace. Now try while running in place or doing jumping jacks. Do this for 3 minutes.

Typical Workout

Ideally you have mastered all of the concepts and training procedures in the previous chapters. Now you want to maintain the strength, flexibility, and stamina, and perception abilities you have built up in your visual system. Following is a short eye workout you can do daily or a few times a week.

Typical Workout*

1. Peripheral expansion chart or sticks and straw #1	3–5 minutes
2. Coin toss with visualization	2–4 minutes
3. Sticks in straw #2	2–4 minutes
4. Four-corner fixation	2–3 minutes
5. Tape on ground	3–5 sets
6. Bug Walk	5 sets
7. Relaxation techniques can be done now now or at other times of the day or week, per week	3–7 times

* Refer to index for page numbers.

You can start this workout with three to seven times a week. If you start 5 to 7 times per week you will attain peak performance sooner, then decrease schedule for maintenance. There may be some procedures that you do less than others if you feel you need them less. Basic maintenance would be as follows.

Basic Maintenance Workout

1. Tape on ground—work on pace, judging distance, tracking abilities. Eliminate jumps and build endurance.	
2. Bug Walk	5 sets
3. Peripheral expansion chart	1/2 to 2 minutes

Pregame Vision Warmup

On the day of a game, you want to be relaxed and confident. Get a good night's sleep, eat properly, and remember a routine improves concentration. Routines are different for different people. Many pros advocate stretching before play and getting there early so you can be relaxed instead of frustrated from running late.

As far as your eyes are concerned, you may find that you do better if you do not do eye exercises before you play. I was a swimmer in school and we never practiced the day of a meet. Doing the string before a game may fatigue your eyes. I suggest doing the peripheral expansion chart and deep breathing before play as these techniques are aimed at getting you into the zone and quieting the mind and body.

One More Tip: Orientation

In any sport whether tennis, baseball, or golf. I tell players to find out where North, South, East and West are in relation to each particular course or field they play on. This helps you feel grounded and oriented in space. This also helps you feel comfortable on the course you are playing.

This chapter includes a sample eye workout schedule. Following are sources for help.

Where to Find Help

College of Optometrists in Vision Development (COVD)
Box 285
Chula Vista, CA 91912-0285
619-425-6191/Fax 619-425-0733

American Optometric Association
Sports Vision Section
243 Lindbergh Blvd.
St. Louis, MO 63141-7881
800-365-2219/Fax 314-991-4101

International Academy of Sports Vision
200 S. Progress Avenue
Harrisburg, PA 17109
717-652-8080/Fax 717-652-8878

Optometric Extension Program Foundation (OEP)
1921 E. Carnegie Ave., Ste. 3-L
Santa Ana, CA 92795-5510
714-250-8070

Call these organizations for a list of doctors in your area. The more organizations the doctor is in, the better. When you call the doctor's office, ask questions pertaining to your needs. Not all doctors do everything involved in sports vision. Some are more expert in sports vision training. Some are more expert in sports injuries for example, and don't do any training programs. Some may fit athletes with contacts and not do training. Some may do training and not do contact lens fittings. So ask questions pertaining to your needs.

Hole in One

Eye workouts, used to train and then maintain your skills, improve:

- Eye teaming skills
- Peripheral vision
- Eye judgment skills
- Visualization skills
- Strength, flexibility, and stamina of the visual system

Chapter  11

Putting It All Together

The main purpose of this chapter is to give you a game plan as to how to use this book. You may feel overwhelmed by all this information and the prospect of doing it all but it will be worth it. I warn every athlete I work with that as they incorporate the concepts and eye workouts into their game, their performance may slip a bit, But when it comes back they reach new levels. It's difficult to change old habits and takes a lot of perseverance to master every step of this book.

Another purpose of this chapter is to give you permission to use as much or as little of this book as you want. As I mentioned earlier, just reading this book and gaining awareness of the concepts will help your consistency.

If It Ain't Broke, Don't Fix It

You may feel that there are areas of your game that are going well for you that you don't want to mess with. Suppose you feel you have no problems judging distance but you're having problems with alignment. Don't alter what you're doing to judge distance. Just master the alignment chapter. In other words, you may just want to use specific chapters that address particular problems you are having. But if you're still not as good as you want to be, take the book out again and do the whole program.

Awareness

Some players improve significantly just by applying a single tip from this program. The following is a list of some of the tips that have been most helpful. They have been previously mentioned.

1. Eye dominance and position over the ball for putting.

2. Eye dominance and whether or not you block one eye on backswing.

3. Using print on ball as a pointer or arrow toward your target.

4. The concept of having a target instead of just hitting the ball.

5. Fine-tuning your vision onto a certain area of the ball when hitting (example: back tip of ball).

6. Running your eyes from the ball to the hole on the greens.

7. Stop looking at the hole right before you stroke your putt.

8. No self-talk when you want to be "in the zone."

9. Specially designed bifocals or not having a bifocal in your golf glasses.

10. Eye alignment (eso or exo) causing problems with judgment.

11. Factoring time into the game (4-second putt).

I was having dinner with a friend who said he was hooking all of his wood shots. I asked him where he looks when he swings. He appeared confuse, like how could I be asking him this and replied, "I look at the ball." I continued, "What part of the ball?" He really had to think. He said, "I guess the top of the ball, I don't know for sure." I interpret these answers as meaning he doesn't really "zoom in" on the ball which means he hasn't fine-tuned his target. I told him to fine-tune on the tip of the ball that the club would hit. Make this a target! He started to hook less almost immediately. He needed to make the target smaller.

Creating New Habits

I have read in books and seen people on TV say it takes 21 days to create a new habit. I've worked with players who improve almost instantly with some "tips" and then go backward again. You must consistently practice the techniques that help you to truly make them your own.

Do the Whole Program

My recommendation for most golfers is to systematically do the whole book. The book is laid out in the order of how you should proceed. Start with the self-test, then go on to alignment, distance, reading the greens, etc. and master the exercises as you go along. This can take months of practice. Remember it takes 21 days to create a new habit. These procedures must be done over and over again. Once you have mastered all of the concepts of the book, keep up your maintenance exercises, especially if you golf all year round.

Re-read the Book

You may pick up more information by re-reading the book once a year especially if you are a seasonal golfer. If you live up north you may want to review the chapters and do the exercises you can do inside starting a couple of months before your golf season. You can develop your own routine. Remember routines aid concentration and consistency.

You Must Have a Target

One of the most important concepts presented here is that you must have a visual target. Think of golf as a target sport except that you have multiple targets. Whether you are on the fairways or the greens remember to assign a visual target to aim for. Don't just look and hit the ball and hope it ends up in a good spot. Pick a target. I have talked about assigning a different target on the greens than the hole. The hole is the goal, but not always the target. Don't look at the hole before you putt, look at the target which may be a spot you use for alignment. The ball itself is also a target. You must strike the ball with the club. You must have a visual target on the ball. We have talked about fine-tuning your vision on the back tip of the ball or the top center of the ball. Do not underestimate the power of having visual targets in golf.

This book will allow you to use your vision in golf. You have an opportunity to master the same programs the pros are doing. Good Luck and Remember....YOU MUST HAVE A TARGET!

Chapter  12

Your Golf Journal

Tracking Progress With Statistics

I want you to keep track of two statistics.

1. Overall score per round.
2. Number of putts per round (very important).

Aside. If you don't play the same number of holes each time out you can track strokes and putts per hole by dividing by number of holes.

Example.

84 strokes on 16 holes

$$\frac{84}{16} \text{ equals } 5\frac{1}{4} \text{ strokes per hole}$$

48 putts on 16 holes

$$\frac{48}{16} = 3 \text{ putts per hole}$$

Let's Record and Graph Our Progress

Strokes per Round (18 holes)

	Date	Score		Date	Score
Game 1	_____	_____	Game 8	_____	_____
2	_____	_____	9	_____	_____
3	_____	_____	10	_____	_____
4	_____	_____	11	_____	_____
5	_____	_____	12	_____	_____
6	_____	_____	13	_____	_____
7	_____	_____	14	_____	_____

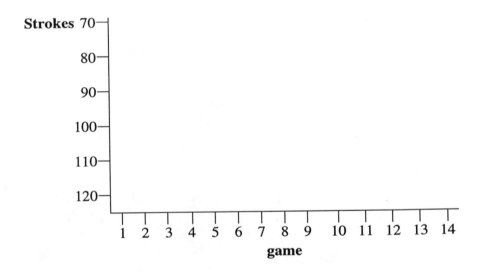

- Place a dot above game number at score
- Connect the dots
- Graph rises as your game improves using this program

Putts Per Round

	Date	# Putts		Date	# Putts
Game 1	_____	_____	Game 8	_____	_____
2	_____	_____	9	_____	_____
3	_____	_____	10	_____	_____
4	_____	_____	11	_____	_____
5	_____	_____	12	_____	_____
6	_____	_____	13	_____	_____
7	_____	_____	14	_____	_____

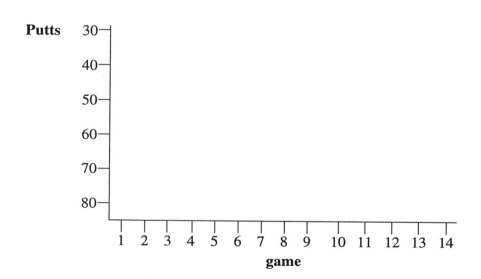

Let's Record and Graph Our Progress

Strokes per Round (18 holes)

	Date	Score		Date	Score
Game 1	_____	_____	Game 8	_____	_____
2	_____	_____	9	_____	_____
3	_____	_____	10	_____	_____
4	_____	_____	11	_____	_____
5	_____	_____	12	_____	_____
6	_____	_____	13	_____	_____
7	_____	_____	14	_____	_____

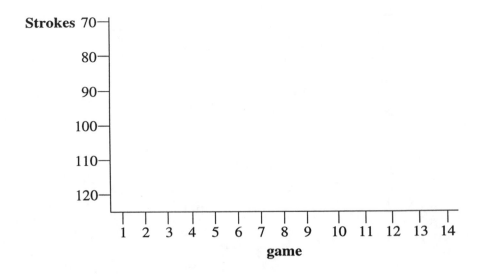

- Place a dot above game number at score
- Connect the dots
- Graph rises as your game improves using this program

Putts Per Round

	Date	# Putts		Date	# Putts
Game 1	_____	_____	Game 8	_____	_____
2	_____	_____	9	_____	_____
3	_____	_____	10	_____	_____
4	_____	_____	11	_____	_____
5	_____	_____	12	_____	_____
6	_____	_____	13	_____	_____
7	_____	_____	14	_____	_____

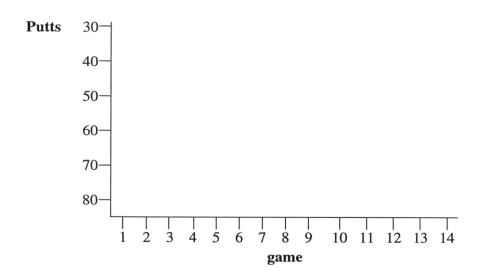

30 Days to Better Golf

Check List

**Sign off when
complete**

1. Read book cover to cover to get basic   _____
   concepts.

2. Do self test and record results (Ch. 3).

   Dominant Eye   R   L   _____
   Eye posture   ortho   exo   eso   _____
                      (circle one)

3. Master alignment (Ch. 4).

   Have friend check putting alignment.   _____

   I was aligned:
   off to right   off to left
        (circle one)

4. Eyes over tape with mirror (p. 36). Study
   this by standing over the line for 20–30
   seconds. Walk away then walk back and
   stand over line 20–30 seconds. Repeat for
   3–5 times. Do at least 3 times per week until
   mastered. Record dates done.

   Week 1   ____ ____ ____ ____ ____ ____ ____

        2   ____ ____ ____ ____ ____ ____ ____

        3   ____ ____ ____ ____ ____ ____ ____

        4   ____ ____ ____ ____ ____ ____ ____

5. Eyes over tape without mirror. Practice putting stroke. Do at least three times per week. Record dates.

Week 1 ____ ____ ____ ____ ____ ____ ____

2 ____ ____ ____ ____ ____ ____ ____

3 ____ ____ ____ ____ ____ ____ ____

4 ____ ____ ____ ____ ____ ____ ____

6. Walk eyes on tape to eliminate jumps. 3–5 times per week or daily (p. 38).

Week 1 ____ ____ ____ ____ ____ ____ ____

2 ____ ____ ____ ____ ____ ____ ____

3 ____ ____ ____ ____ ____ ____ ____

4 ____ ____ ____ ____ ____ ____ ____

7. Distance (Ch. 5).

Master distance with tape on ground with markings. Practice 3–7 times per week.

Week 1 ____ ____ ____ ____ ____ ____ ____

2 ____ ____ ____ ____ ____ ____ ____

3 ____ ____ ____ ____ ____ ____ ____

4 ____ ____ ____ ____ ____ ____ ____

**Sign off when
complete**

8. Master distance judgment exercises without   _____
    tape (Ch. 5). Do whenever and wherever
    you can.

9. Eye exercises (Ch. 6). Practice and master
    the string.

    Triple bead, 3–5 times a week.

Week 1   ____   ____   ____   ____   ____   ____   ____

     2   ____   ____   ____   ____   ____   ____   ____

     3   ____   ____   ____   ____   ____   ____   ____

     4   ____   ____   ____   ____   ____   ____   ____

    Bug walk, 3–5 times a week.

Week 1   ____   ____   ____   ____   ____   ____   ____

     2   ____   ____   ____   ____   ____   ____   ____

     3   ____   ____   ____   ____   ____   ____   ____

     4   ____   ____   ____   ____   ____   ____   ____

10. Do stick and straw 3–5 times per week.

Week 1   ____   ____   ____   ____   ____   ____   ____

     2   ____   ____   ____   ____   ____   ____   ____

     3   ____   ____   ____   ____   ____   ____   ____

     4   ____   ____   ____   ____   ____   ____   ____

11. Peripheral expansion 3–5 times per week.

Week 1 ____ ____ ____ ____ ____ ____ ____

2 ____ ____ ____ ____ ____ ____ ____

3 ____ ____ ____ ____ ____ ____ ____

4 ____ ____ ____ ____ ____ ____ ____

12. Coin toss 3–5 times per week.

Week 1 ____ ____ ____ ____ ____ ____ ____

2 ____ ____ ____ ____ ____ ____ ____

3 ____ ____ ____ ____ ____ ____ ____

4 ____ ____ ____ ____ ____ ____ ____

13. Four-corner fixation 3–5 times per week.

Week 1 ____ ____ ____ ____ ____ ____ ____

2 ____ ____ ____ ____ ____ ____ ____

3 ____ ____ ____ ____ ____ ____ ____

4 ____ ____ ____ ____ ____ ____ ____

14. Mind-body calming technique (Ch. 8). 5
    times per week.

Week 1 ___ ___ ___ ___ ___ ___ ___

    2 ___ ___ ___ ___ ___ ___ ___

    3 ___ ___ ___ ___ ___ ___ ___

    4 ___ ___ ___ ___ ___ ___ ___

15. Visualization and observation and closed
    eye procedure (Ch. 8). 3–5 times per week.

Week 1 ___ ___ ___ ___ ___ ___ ___

    2 ___ ___ ___ ___ ___ ___ ___

    3 ___ ___ ___ ___ ___ ___ ___

    4 ___ ___ ___ ___ ___ ___ ___

If you do not have a lot of time do half of above one day and other
half the next. If you spend 3–5 minutes per activity you can do all of
these plus tape work in under 50 minutes. Again, you do not have to
do them all if you don't feel you have a problem with a particular area.

On the Golf Course

**Sign off when
complete**

1. Develop a routine.   _____

2. Concentrate on staying in the visual zone.   _____

3. Practice putting on each green from three   _____
   different starting points and distances.

4. Have pro read greens with you.   _____

5. Study speed and time of putts.   _____

6. Master plumb bob.   _____

7. Re-putt same shot over and over to learn to   _____
   assign a different visual target for putting.

8. Visualize shots before you make them.   _____

Before the Game

1. Peripheral Expansion Chart
2. Deep Breathing

Typical Eye Workout Chart (fill in dates done)

Exercise	Date	Date	Date	Date	Date	Date	Date	Date	Date	Date	Date	Date	Date	Date	Date
1. Peripheral expansion 3 minutes															
2. Coin toss with visualization 2–4 minutes															
3. Stick in straw 3–4 minutes															
4. Four corner fixation 2–3 minutes															
5. Tape on ground 3 minutes															
6. Bug walk 5 sets															
7. Relaxation techniques															

Typical Eye Workout Chart (fill in dates done)

	Date	Date	Date	Date	Date	Date	Date	Date	Date	Date	Date	Date	Date	Date
1. Peripheral expansion 3 minutes														
2. Coin toss with visualization 2–4 minutes														
3. Stick in straw 3–4 minutes														
4. Four corner fixation 2–3 minutes														
5. Tape on ground 3 minutes														
6. Bug walk 5 sets														
7. Relaxation techniques														

Typical Eye Workout Chart (fill in dates done)

	Date	Date	Date	Date	Date	Date	Date	Date	Date	Date	Date	Date	Date	Date
1. Peripheral expansion 3 minutes														
2. Coin toss with visualization 2–4 minutes														
3. Stick in straw 3–4 minutes														
4. Four corner fixation 2–3 minutes														
5. Tape on ground 3 minutes														
6. Bug walk 5 sets														
7. Relaxation techniques														

Basic Maintenance Workout Check-Off Sheet (fill in dates done)

	Date	Date	Date	Date	Date	Date	Date	Date	Date	Date	Date	Date	Date	Date
1. Tape on ground 3–5 minutes														
2. Bug walk 5 sets														
3. Peripheral expansion chart 1½–2 minutes														

Basic Maintenance Workout Check-Off Sheet (fill in dates done)

	Date	Date	Date	Date	Date	Date	Date	Date	Date	Date	Date	Date	Date	Date	Date
1. Tape on ground 3–5 minutes															
2. Bug walk 5 sets															
3. Peripheral expansion chart 1½–2 minutes															

Basic Maintenance Workout Check-Off Sheet (fill in dates done)

	Date	Date	Date	Date	Date	Date	Date	Date	Date	Date	Date	Date	Date	Date
1. Tape on ground 3–5 minutes														
2. Bug walk 5 sets														
3. Peripheral expansion chart 1½–2 minutes														

About the Author

Dr. Lampert was first introduced to sports vision training in 1984 when he interned in the practice that trained the Philadelphia Flyers in areas such as eye movement skills, eye-hand coordination, visual memory, side vision awareness, and many more areas important to a hockey player's visual performance.

Today he has a successful practice in Boca Raton, FL where well over 50 percent of his time goes to providing specialty care in the forms of vision rehabilitation for stroke and head injury victims, treatment of children and adults with binocular dysfunctions (these are problems where the eyes do not work well as a team, lose their focus, and do not land on the right place), and designing and delivering Sports Vision Training programs for professional and amateur athletes.

He has worked with players from the Yankees, Cubs, and Dolphins, professional golfers and tennis players, weekend warriors, and school teams. He was a member of the team of vision specialists screening Olympic athletes at Bausch and Lomb's Olympic Vision Performance center in Atlanta at the 1996 Summer games.

Index

A

accommodation, eye. *see*
    focusing
affirmations, 94
aging golfers. *see* older golfers
Alvarez, Judy, 12, 62
astigmatism, 62, 101, 102–103,
    105
awareness of visual system, 4,
    126–127

B

Ballesteros, Seve, 18
Berning, Susie Maxwell, 61
bifocals, 5, 101, 103, 106–107,
    108
brain/visual system connection,
    84
bug walk, 63–65, 114–115

C

Coffey, Dr. Bradley, 11
concentration, 7, 87–88
consistency, 95
contacts, 105–106
contact with ball, 16
contours, reading, 1
contrast sensitivity, 6
Crenshaw, Ben, 18

D

depth perception, 1, 3
    definition, 6
    importance to golfers with
        one eye weaker than
        other, 6–7
distance
    adjustments for in putting, 78
    factoring time, 57–58, 126

judging, 51, 53–54
pacing training, 55
tape training, 54–55
three-foot circle concept,
    52–53
Dooly, Vince, 11
downhill putting. *see* putting
driving,,7
alignment technique for,
    46–47
dynamic visual acuity, 3, 7

E

elevated rim cup, 80
Elkington, Steve, 12
Endicott, Lori, 12
esophoria. *see* eye alignment
exercises, eye. *see* eye muscle
    training exercises
exophoria. *see* eye alignment
eye-aiming, 3
eye alignment, 2, 4–5, 8, 126
    from address position, 34
    ball as alignment tool, 42–43,
        126
    changes during times of stress,
        25
    club shaft technique, 41–42
    definition, 19–20
    esophoria, 20, 22, 54
        behavior predictions, 25
    exophoria, 20, 21, 22, 48, 54
        behavior predictions,
            24–26
    full swing, 46–49
    for long putts, 40–41
    measuring, 23–24

orthophoria, 20
    behavior predictions,
        25–26
painted putter technique, 44
position over ball, 35
putter heads for measuring,
    33–34
for short chips, 44–46
for short putts, 40
stabilizing, 25
strengthening, 25
tape, running eyes along,
    technique, 38–40
tape and mirror technique,
    36–38
tape technique, 35–36
target, making smaller, 43
test, 20–22, 34–35
eye chart, 104
eye dominance, 3, 4, 126
    cross-dominance, 16, 18–19,
        38, 67–69
    definition, 15–16
    same-side dominance, 16, 19
    test one, 16
    test three, 17–1818
    test two, 17–18
eyeglasses
    bifocals. *see* bifocals
    contacts. *see* contacts
    lenses, 104–105, 106
    photochromatic lenses, 109
    prescriptions, 7, 106
    sunglasses, 108–109
eye-hand coordination, 1, 3
    reaction time, 7–8
eye movements
    accuracy, 1
    pursuits, 5

saccade, 5
smoothness of, 5
speed, 1, 2, 3
eye muscle training exercises
    bug walk, 63–65, 114–115
    coin toss, 117–118
    four-corner fixations, 119–120
    one bead on a string, 112–113
    stick and straw #1, 65–66
    sticks in straw #2, 119
    string, the, 111–112
    three beads on a string,
        113–114
    typical workout, 120–122
eye stamina, 8
eye suppression, 64–65
    test, 26–29
eye teaming, 6, 8
eye tests, sports vision training.
        see sports vision
        training
eye workout, typical, 120–122

F

Faldo, Nick, 12, 34, 88
Farnsworth,Dr. Craig, 12
farsightedness, 62, 101, 102
Floyd, Raymond, 18
focusing, 1, 5–6
four-corner fixations, 119–120

G

greens
    Bermuda grass, 72

breaks, 61, 68
dry, 79
fast, 79
grains, 6, 68, 72
just noticeable differences, 62
reading, 4, 5, 6, 9, 16, 61
    pro lesson, advantage to,
        70, 72
slow, 79
"walking" eyes across, 62–63
wet, 79

H

habits, creating new ones, 127

J

Jabbar, Kareem Abdul, 11
JNDs. *see* just noticeable
        differences
Johnson, Howard, 11
Jordan, Patty, 19
judgment of location, 1, 2
just noticeable differences, 62

K

Kite, Tom, 12, 18

L

Lowe, Dr. Sue, 11

M

myopia. *see* nearsightedness

N

navigation and vector principles, 75–78
nearsightedness, 25, 101–102
Nicklaus, Jack, 18

O

older golfers, 5–6, 7, 62
Olesky, Walter, 87
Olympic atheletes, visual skills, 2–3
one bead on a string exercise, 112–113
orthophoria. *see* eye alignment

P

Palmer, Arnold, 18
peripheral vision, 7, 115, 117–118
   expansion exercises, 65–66, 115, 117–118
photochromatic eyeglass lenses, 109
plumb bob, 67–69
presbyopia, 103
prism diopter, 23
Purdy, Ted, 12
putting
   analyzing speed, 57
   assigning a length, 80
   assigning a target, 75, 78, 82
   breaks, 79–84
   consistency, 16, 56
   distance adjustments, 78
   downhill, 57, 78, 79
   level, 75, 78
   long, 40–41, 52, 56, 57
   making target smaller, 52–53
   navigation and vector principles, 75–78
   referencing to level, 82
   routine, 88–89
   short, 40, 56
   uphill, 57, 78, 79, 82

R

reading greens. *see* greens
Reed, Jake, 12
relaxation, 2, 7
   techniques, 91–93
routine, establishing for putting. *see* putting
Rudolf, Mason, 61–62
Runninger, Jack, O.D., 61

S

self-talk, 89, 91, 97, 126
senior citizen golfers. *see* older golfers
sensory systems, relationship to the zone. *see* "zone, the"
Skinner, Val, 11, 19, 25
spatial localization, 6
sports vision training

golf pros who utilize, 11–12
importance to golf game, 8
specialists, listings of
        organizations, 122–123
sports utilized in, 1, 2,
        11–12
success stories, 9
tests, 20–22, 26–29
Stadler, Craig, 18
stance, 18
    for cross-dominant golfers,
        38
static visual acuity, 7
sticks in straw #1, 65–66
sticks in straw #2, 119
sunglasses, 108–109
swing
    full, 46–49
    pendulum, 56

T

targets
    assigning, 2
Teig, Dr. Donald, 22
three beads on a string exercise,
        113–114
three-foot circle concept,
        52–53

U

uphill putting. *see* putting
UVA rays, 108

UVB rays, 108
UVC rays, 108

V

Vanderwege, Kiki, 11
20/20 vision, 7, 102, 103, 105
visual energy, 93–94
visualization
    closed-eye, 97
    for consistent swing, 95
    definition, 94–95
    difficulties, 98
    skills, 3
    techniques, 96–97
visual system/brain connection,
        84

W

Wadkins, Bobby, 12
Watson, Tom, 18
workout, eye, 120–122

Z

"zone, the," 1, 8, 87, 126
    definition, 89
    relaxation techniques. *see*
        relaxation
    sensory systems, relationship
        between, 89–91
    visualization. *see* visualization

Saturn Press

Order These Other Exciting Titles From Saturn Press

As seen on GMA, MSNBC, and the Gayle King Show!

KATHY LEVINSON, PH.D.

1-88584-304-6 • $12.95(p) Sept

FIRST AID FOR TANTRUMS
Kathy Levinson, Ph.D.

Family therapist and school psychologist Kathy Levinson offers effective strategies for dealing with children's tantrums, from the terrible two's through the turbulent teens. Learn the most common tantrum triggers, when a tantrum is not a tantrum, if time-out really works, and how to handle plane trips, long car rides, the supermarket, and more.

SKIN CARE
Clear & Simple
Ligaya H. Buchbinder, M.D.

Noted dermatologist Ligaya Buchbinder may not have found the fountain of youth, but she is close to certain that she has slowed her own aging process. Buchbinder helps readers tailor a skin care regimen that works because it is tailored to *their* individual skin conditions. Learn the latest trends in skin care, learn which moisturizers, revitalizers and treatments work...and which don't. Turn back your aging process!

1-88584-305-4 • $12.95(p) Oct

As seen on the FOX News Channel

1-88584-301-1 • $7.95(p) Sept

A MOTHER'S WISDOM
Anne Marie Walsh

Brimming with common sense, down-to-earth advice and heartfelt anecdotes, this lovely book touches a chord in every parent who may doubt his or her own ability to raise children in our fast-paced, complicated world.

As seen in Vogue and Fitness

For Trade Orders, Call 1-800-462-6420.
Available at your favorite bookstore or call 1-888-32BOOKS.
Prices do not reflect shipping & handling charges.

Saturn Press • 17639 Foxborough Lane • Boca Raton FL 33496

 Saturn Press

Order These Other Exciting Titles From Saturn Press

1-88584307-0 • $12.95(p) May

THE VIEW FROM MY HOUSE
JoAnn Baker

New York syndicated columnist
and mother of two, Baker shares
funny, candid stories about family life in the 90's.

THE BIG SLEEP:
True Tales & Twisted Facts about
Death
Erica Orloff
JoAnn Baker

1-88584309-7 • Oct

Here's a book that will both in-
trigue and fascinate you. It contains facts you wouldn't know,
stories you couldn't know, and
accounts you shouldn't know.

1-88584306-2 • $14.95(p) May

THE PRO'S EDGE
Vision Training for Golf
Dr. Lawrence D. Lampert

Vision training is the hottest talk
in pro sports today. With the same
techniques he uses with the pros,
let Dr. Lampert teach you how to
change your game forever.

A MATTER OF HEART:
One Woman's Story of Triumph
Nancy Pedder

1-88584308-9 • Oct

A beautifully told story of one
woman's determination to survive
both breast cancer and a heart
transplant. Underscores the price-
less gift of organ donation.

For Trade Orders, Call 1-800-462-6420.
Available at your favorite bookstore or call 1-888-32BOOKS.
Prices do not reflect shipping & handling charges.

Saturn Press • 17639 Foxborough Lane • Boca Raton FL 33496